D0856111

Private Property
Rights

Affirmative Action
Amateur Athletics
American Military Policy
Animal Rights
Capital Punishment
DNA Evidence
Educational Standards
Election Reform
The FCC and Regulating Indecency
Fetal Rights
Freedom of Speech
Gay Rights
Gun Control
Immigrants' Rights After 9/11
Immigration Policy
Legalizing Marijuana
Mandatory Military Service
Media Bias
Mental Health Reform
Miranda Rights
Open Government
Physician-Assisted Suicide
Policing the Internet
Prisoners' Rights
Private Property Rights
Protecting Ideas
Religion in Public Schools
Rights of Students
The Right to Die
The Right to Privacy
Search and Seizure
Smoking Bans
Stem Cell Research and Cloning
Tort Reform
Trial of Juveniles as Adults
The War on Terror
Welfare Reform
Women in the Military

Private Property Rights

Paul Ruschmann, J.D.
and
Maryanne Nasiatka

SERIES CONSULTING EDITOR
Alan Marzilli, M.A., J.D.

CHELSEA HOUSE
PUBLISHERS
An imprint of Infobase Publishing

Private Property Rights

Chelsea House
An imprint of Infobase Publishing
132 West 31st Street
New York, NY 10001

Library of Congress Cataloging-in-Publication Data

Ruschmann, Paul.
  Private property rights / Paul Ruschmann, and Maryanne Nasiatka.
    p. cm. — (Point/counterpoint)
  Includes bibliographical references and index.
  ISBN-13: 978-0-7910-9520-1 (hardcover)
  ISBN-10: 0-7910-9520-7 (hardcover)
  1. Right of property—United States. 2. Land use—Law and legislation—United States. 3. Zoning law—United States. I. Nasiatka, Maryanne. II. Title. III. Series.

  KF562.R87 2007
  346.7304'4—dc22   2007003657

CONTENTS

Foreword   6

INTRODUCTION
Is Your Home Really Your Castle?   10

POINT
The Government Abuses Condemnation   24

COUNTERPOINT
Condemnation Promotes the Public Welfare   37

POINT
Land-use Restrictions Are Unjust to
Property Owners   49

COUNTERPOINT
Land-use Restrictions Are in the
Public Interest   61

POINT
Zoning Harms Property Owners and
Provides Few Benefits to Society   74

COUNTERPOINT
Zoning Promotes Better Communities   86

CONCLUSION
The Future of Private Property Rights   102

Notes   118
Resources   122
Elements of the Argument   124
Appendix: Beginning Legal Research   127
Index   131

Foreword

Alan Marzilli, M.A., J.D.
Washington, D.C.

The debates presented in POINT/COUNTERPOINT are among the most interesting and controversial in contemporary American society, but studying them is more than an academic activity. They affect every citizen; they are the issues that today's leaders debate and tomorrow's will decide. The reader may one day play a central role in resolving them.

Why study both sides of the debate? It's possible that the reader will not yet have formed any opinion at all on the subject of this volume—but this is unlikely. It is more likely that the reader will already hold an opinion, probably a strong one, and very probably one formed without full exposure to the arguments of the other side. It is rare to hear an argument presented in a balanced way, and it is easy to form an opinion on too little information; these books will help to fill in the informational gaps that can never be avoided. More important, though, is the practical function of the series: Skillful argumentation requires a thorough knowledge of *both* sides—though there are seldom only two, and only by knowing what an opponent is likely to assert can one form an articulate response.

Perhaps more important is that listening to the other side sometimes helps one to see an opponent's arguments in a more human way. For example, Sister Helen Prejean, one of the nation's most visible opponents of capital punishment, has been deeply affected by her interactions with the families of murder victims. Seeing the families' grief and pain, she understands much better why people support the death penalty, and she is able to carry out her advocacy with a greater sensitivity to the needs and beliefs of those who do not agree with her. Her relativism, in turn, lends credibility to her work. Dismissing the other side of the argument as totally without merit can be too easy—it is far more useful to understand the nature of the controversy and the reasons *why* the issue defies resolution.

The most controversial issues of all are often those that center on a constitutional right. The Bill of Rights—the first ten amendments to the U.S. Constitution—spells out some of the most fundamental rights that distinguish the governmental system of the United States from those that allow fewer (or other) freedoms. But the sparsely worded document is open to interpretation, and clauses of only a few words are often at the heart of national debates. The Bill of Rights was meant to protect individual liberties; but the needs of some individuals clash with those of society as a whole, and when this happens someone has to decide where to draw the line. Thus the Constitution becomes a battleground between the rights of individuals to do as they please and the responsibility of the government to protect its citizens. The First Amendment's guarantee of "freedom of speech," for example, leads to a number of difficult questions. Some forms of expression, such as burning an American flag, lead to public outrage—but nevertheless are said to be protected by the First Amendment. Other types of expression that most people find objectionable, such as sexually explicit material involving children, are not protected because they are considered harmful. The question is not only where to draw the line, but how to do this without infringing on the personal liberties on which the United States was built.

The Bill of Rights raises many other questions about individual rights and the societal "good." Is a prayer before a high school football game an "establishment of religion" prohibited by the First Amendment? Does the Second Amendment's promise of "the right to bear arms" include concealed handguns? Is stopping and frisking someone standing on a corner known to be frequented by drug dealers a form of "unreasonable search and seizure" in violation of the Fourth Amendment? Although the nine-member U.S. Supreme Court has the ultimate authority in interpreting the Constitution, its answers do not always satisfy the public. When a group of nine people—sometimes by a five-to-four vote—makes a decision that affects the lives of hundreds of millions, public outcry can be expected. And the composition of the Court does change over time, so even a landmark decision is not guaranteed to stand forever. The limits of constitutional protection are always in flux.

These issues make headlines, divide courts, and decide elections. They are the questions most worthy of national debate, and this series aims to cover them as thoroughly as possible. Each volume sets out some of the key arguments surrounding a particular issue, even some views that most people consider extreme or radical—but presents a balanced perspective on the issue. Excerpts from the relevant laws and judicial opinions and references to central concepts, source material, and advocacy groups help the reader to explore the issues even further and to read "the letter of the law" just as the legislatures and the courts have established it.

It may seem that some debates—such as those over capital punishment and abortion, debates with a strong moral component—will never be resolved. But American history offers numerous examples of controversies that once seemed insurmountable but now are effectively settled, even if only on the surface. Abolitionists met with widespread resistance to their efforts to end slavery, and the controversy over that issue threatened to cleave the nation in two; but today public debate over the merits of slavery would be unthinkable, though racial inequalities still plague the nation. Similarly unthinkable at one time was suffrage for women and minorities, but this is now a matter of course. Distributing information about contraception once was a crime. Societies change, and attitudes change, and new questions of social justice are raised constantly while the old ones fade into irrelevancy.

Whatever the root of the controversy, the books in POINT/ COUNTERPOINT seek to explain to the reader the origins of the debate, the current state of the law, and the arguments on both sides. The goal of the series is to inform the reader about the issues facing not only American politicians, but all of the nation's citizens, and to encourage the reader to become more actively involved in resolving these debates, as a voter, a concerned citizen, a journalist, an activist, or an elected official. Democracy is based on education, and every voice counts—so every opinion must be an informed one.

———•———————•————————•———

One of the hallmarks of a free society is that individuals have the right to own property, rather than a monarch or central government controlling all of a nation's land. The founders of the United States believed that one's home is one's castle, but in the U.S. Constitution they acknowledged that, under certain circumstances, the government would have reason to take a landowner's property. Therefore, the Constitution provides protection to landowners in these situations. Generally, the Constitution requires the government to allow landowners to contest the government's taking of property; when the government does take property, it must provide just compensation. A recent decision by the U.S. Supreme Court interpreting this section of the Constitution generated a national controversy: The Court ruled that a Connecticut city could take away a woman's house and give it to a private company that was turning her neighborhood into a commercial development.

In addition to placing limits on governmental seizure of property, courts have held that the U.S. and state constitutions limit the governments' abilities to restrict landowners' use of their land. Two of the ways that governments regulate land use are through environmental laws, which regulate building and commercial activity to protect air, water, and animal habitats; and local zoning laws, which regulate building size and the types of use for certain properties—for example, prohibiting an all-night dance club in a residential neighborhood.

Private Property Rights examines the controversies outlined above: For which purposes may the government take a person's land? Should the government regulate land use for the common good, or should individual property owners have complete sovereignty over the land they own?

Is Your Home Really Your Castle?

The United States Supreme Court's most controversial decisions typically involve emotional issues such as gay rights, the death penalty, and the fight against terrorism. That was not true of the Court's 2004–2005 term. Its most-debated ruling from that term came in a case that involved the scope of the government's power to condemn property—that is, force the owner to sell his or her property so that it can be reused on behalf of the public. The case turned on technical issues of constitutional law that normally would attract little interest outside the legal community. The story behind this case, however, garnered national attention.

A Woman's Fight to Save Her Home

The case of *Kelo v. City of New London*, 545 U.S. 469 (2005), began when city officials in New London, Connecticut, con-

Susette Kelo's house in the Fort Trumbull section of New London, Connecticut, is shown above. New London city officials attempted to seize Kelo's home, along with several others nearby, under the state's privilege of eminent domain.

cluded that steps needed to be taken to revive the sagging local economy. They approved a redevelopment plan that involved replacing portions of the aging downtown and waterfront district with a research facility for the drug maker Pfizer, Inc., along with shops and restaurants, new homes, and parkland. In their view, the redevelopment would create jobs and revitalize the local economy.

In order to redevelop the area, the city had to acquire the property and then turn it over to a private company that would actually do the development. Most of the owners in the area agreed to sell their property, but some refused. One of the holdouts was Susette Kelo, who did not want to leave the small century-old home that she had recently refurbished. The city then moved to condemn her home. People commonly associate the word "condemned" with a dilapidated structure that must be torn down. Kelo's home was not dilapidated, nor had she had broken any laws or fallen behind in paying her property taxes.

Susette Kelo's supporters portrayed her as the victim of uncaring politicians and greedy developers. She faced eviction from her home merely because city officials thought that someone else would make better use of her property. Organizations that were formed to defend property rights found lawyers

FROM THE BENCH

What the *Kelo* Majority Wrote

Kelo v. City of New London was decided by a 5 to 4 vote. In his majority opinion, Justice John Paul Stevens noted that, in the past, the Court had defined "public purpose" broadly, "reflecting our longstanding policy of deference to legislative judgments in this field." He wrote:

> Viewed as a whole, our jurisprudence has recognized that the needs of society have varied between different parts of the Nation, just as they have evolved over time in response to changed circumstances. Our earliest cases in particular embodied a strong theme of federalism, emphasizing the "great respect" that we owe to state legislatures and state courts in discerning local public needs. . . . For more than a century, our public use jurisprudence has wisely eschewed rigid formulas and intrusive scrutiny in favor of affording legislatures broad latitude in determining what public needs justify the use of the takings power.

Justice Stevens insisted that economic development met the public-use requirement and described it as "a traditional and long accepted function of government." Susette Kelo's lawyers argued that permitting economic-benefit condemnations would justify "transferring citizen A's property to citizen B for the sole reason that citizen B will put the property to a more productive use and thus pay more taxes," but Justice Stevens called that argument "hypothetical" and stated that the Court would confront it if and when it arose.

Justice Stevens also rejected the argument that officials must justify a proposed condemnation by showing a "reasonable certainty" that the public benefits would materialize. He refused to question their predictions about the project's economic

to represent her and told her story to the country. Kelo soon became the symbol of the fight against condemnation abuse.

In court, Kelo's lawyers argued that the condemnation of her property violated the Takings Clause of the Fifth Amendment of the United States Constitution, which reads, "nor shall private property be taken for public use, without just compensation."[1] They contended that the city would not put her property to a "public use" after acquiring it but would instead turn it over to another private owner.

impact or their determination as to how much land was needed for the project. He also observed that condemnation might be more necessary in older cities such as New London, where centuries of development had created "an extreme overdivision of land" that made it very difficult to assemble the necessary parcels of land.

Finally, Justice Stevens invited property-rights advocates to work at the state and local level to roll back condemnation powers. He wrote:

> We emphasize that nothing in our opinion precludes any State from placing further restrictions on its exercise of the takings power. Indeed, many States already impose "public use" requirements that are stricter than the federal baseline. Some of these requirements have been established as a matter of state constitutional law, while others are expressed in state eminent domain statutes that carefully limit the grounds upon which takings may be exercised.

Although he agreed with Justice Stevens's reasoning, Justice Anthony Kennedy wrote a concurring opinion that added several observations of his own. He emphasized that courts should find a taking unconstitutional when it was clear that it was intended to benefit a specific private party. In this case, however, the intent of the development plan was to benefit the entire community, not just Pfizer, Inc., or the developer of the project. Justice Kennedy also cautioned that an outright ban, or stringent restrictions on, economic-development condemnations would prohibit many takings that would confer "substantial benefits on the public at large." In this case, he noted that New London had drawn up a comprehensive plan meant to address a city-wide depression and had complied with "elaborate procedural requirements" meant to ensure openness and honesty.

The lawsuit reached the Supreme Court which, by a 5 to 4 majority, concluded that New London's redevelopment project met the Takings Clause's public-use requirement. The Court ruled that it was up to state and local officials, not the courts, to determine whether condemnation would further a public purpose. Accordingly, it accepted at face value the city's determination that the project would add jobs and increase the city's tax base. In doing so, the justices followed the reasoning of two earlier decisions that recognized broad condemnation power, also known as the *eminent domain* power. The first was *Berman v. Parker*, 348 U.S. 26 (1954), which cleared the way for an urban-renewal project that involved the condemnation of hundreds of buildings in a blighted urban neighborhood. The second was *Hawaii Housing Authority v. Midkiff*, 467 U.S. 229 (1984), which affirmed state lawmakers' use of condemnation to break up huge landholdings.

The *Kelo* decision is consistent with the modern Supreme Court's approach toward a state government's exercise of its police power—that is, its power to enact "what measures are appropriate or needful for the protection of the public morals, the public health, or the public safety."[2] Since the late 1930s, the Court's approach has been deferential, or "hands-off." The language it used in a 1938 decision is typical:

> Regulatory legislation affecting ordinary commercial transactions is not to be pronounced unconstitutional unless, in the light of the facts made known or generally assumed, it is of such a character as to preclude the assumption that it rests upon some rational basis within the knowledge and experience of the legislators.[3]

In *Midkiff*, the Court ruled that it would take a deferential approach toward condemnation cases as well. It stated that "the 'public use' requirement is thus coterminous with [has the same limits as] the scope of a sovereign's police powers."[4] Many state courts have similarly taken a deferential approach and have upheld condemnation for a wide variety of reasons, including economic-development projects similar to the one in *Kelo*. The most famous state court decision was *Poletown Neighborhood Council v. City of Detroit*, 410 Mich. 616, 304 N.W.2d 455 (Mich. Sup. Ct. 1981), in which the Supreme Court of Michigan upheld the condemnation of an entire neighborhood in Detroit so that General Motors Corporation could build an assembly plant there.

In Condemning Property, Does Government Go Too Far?

The four dissenters in *Kelo*, led by Justice Sandra Day O'Connor, argued that economic-development condemnations did not meet the public-use requirement. They insisted that New London was simply taking land from one private citizen and turning it over to another without any *direct* benefit to the public. The dissenters also warned that the majority's broad reading of the public-use requirement left no limits on the government's power to condemn property.

The dissenters also maintained that the majority had given the government even broader eminent domain power than the *Berman* and *Midkiff* courts. They pointed out that the condemnations in *Berman* were used to rid the city of blighted structures and those in *Midkiff* were aimed at ending a system of land ownership that harmed the public. In *Kelo*, however, the only "harm" that resulted from Susette Kelo's use of her property was city officials' belief that she was not using it profitably enough. Justice O'Connor warned that, if the government could take property for that reason, other abuses would follow. She wrote,

> [W]ho among us can say she already makes the most productive or attractive possible use of her property? The specter of condemnation hangs over all property. Nothing is to prevent the State from replacing any Motel 6 with a Ritz-Carlton, any home with a shopping mall, or any farm with a factory.[5]

Justice Clarence Thomas, who also wrote a dissenting opinion, took an even more restrictive view of the government's condemnation power. He maintained that the Court had mis-read the Takings Clause in *Berman* and *Midkiff* and strayed even farther from the intent of the Framers of the Constitution in *Kelo*.

Drawing the Line Between Regulations and Takings

Centuries-old legal principles support the claim that there are limits to the government's power to interfere with prop-

Urban Renewal Found Constitutional: *Berman v. Parker*

In 1945, Congress passed a redevelopment act for the District of Columbia. The act created a land agency that had the power to acquire property, by condemnation if necessary, and a planning commission that was responsible for drawing up a master plan.

The first major project was the redevelopment of a neighborhood in the south-west portion of the district where 5,000 people lived. Sixty-four percent of the dwellings there were "beyond repair," and a large majority lacked basic amenities such as indoor toilets, bathtubs, and central heating. The redevelopment plan called for widespread condemnation of buildings to make way for a new neigh-borhood.

One of those buildings was a department store owned by Max Morris. Sam Berman, who represented Morris's estate, filed suit to block the store's con-demnation. He argued that, because the store was not a blighted property, the public-use requirement barred the district from taking it. Berman's lawsuit went to the United States Supreme Court, which, in *Berman v. Parker*, 348 U.S. 26 (1954), unanimously ruled in favor of the district. Justice William O. Douglas wrote the majority opinion.

Justice Douglas concluded that the redevelopment plan was an exercise of the district's police power and pointed out that the Court applied a deferential stan-dard toward such exercises. He wrote, "The definition is essentially the product of legislative determinations addressed to the purposes of government, purposes neither abstractly nor historically capable of complete definition. Subject to

erty rights. An early effort to curb that power was the Magna Carta, which King John of England signed in 1215. A section of that document provided, "No freemen shall be taken or imprisoned or disseised [lose their land] or exiled or in any way destroyed, nor will we go upon him nor send upon him, except by the lawful judgment of his peers or by the law of the land."[6]

The notions that not even the king is above the law and that citizens have God-given rights—including property rights—

specific constitutional limitations, when the legislature has spoken, the public interest has been declared in terms well-nigh conclusive."

He next concluded that the same deferential standard applied to condemnations as well: If the government's objective was permissible, then the condemnation of property was an appropriate means to achieve that end. Justice Douglas also observed that the concept of public welfare was "broad and inclusive" enough to permit the district to create attractive, as well as safe, neighborhoods.

Although the redevelopment plan would transfer property from one private owner to another, Justice Douglas concluded that such a transfer would promote the public welfare. He added that the government could attack the problem of urban blight on an area-wide basis rather than on a structure-by-structure basis. In this case, he noted, the district's experts had concluded that a comprehensive plan was needed to make sure that the area would not become blighted once again. He wrote in response to property owners such as Berman, "If owner after owner were permitted to resist these redevelopment programs on the ground that his particular property was not being used against the public interest, integrated plans for redevelopment would suffer greatly."

Although the *Berman* Court held that large-scale urban-renewal projects were constitutional, many turned out to be failures. Condemned neighborhoods were often replaced by huge and ugly public housing projects that quickly turned into slums themselves. Eventually, government planners abandoned the idea. The demolition of the huge Pruitt-Igoe housing project in St. Louis in 1974 marked a symbolic end of the housing-project era. Nevertheless, redevelopment lived on and planners went forward with other development projects that had little to do with slum clearance.

influenced the Framers of the Constitution, who wrote the Takings Clause into the Bill of Rights.

Legal scholars believe that James Madison, who wrote the Takings Clause, intended that it apply only to physical takings, not to regulations that deprived the owner of the use or value of his or her property. The Supreme Court took that approach in *Mugler v. Kansas*, 123 U.S. 623 (1887), in which it rejected a brewery owner's claim that the state had denied him due process of law by enacting Prohibition. The Court reasoned that prohibiting the sale of beer was a legitimate exercise of the state's police powers. The brewery owner therefore was not entitled to compensation, even though the law had reduced the value of his property by 75 percent. Later decisions applied the same reasoning to government actions that shut down a brickyard and a gravel and sand mine and that ordered the owner of cedar trees to destroy them in order to prevent the spread of disease.

In *Pennsylvania Coal Company v. Mahon*, 260 U.S. 393 (1922), however, the Supreme Court opened the door to lawsuits that claimed that a "regulatory taking" had occurred. In *Mahon*, the justices held that a state law that banned the mining of coal underneath homes deprived the coal company of property and contract rights and thus amounted to a taking of its property. Decades later, in *Penn Central Transportation Company v. New York City*, 438 U.S. 104 (1978), the Court revisited the issue of regulatory takings. Although it upheld New York City's historic-preservation ordinance, the justices stated that a land-use regulation could deprive the owner of the entire value of his property and thus amount to a taking.

In the years that followed, the Court handed down a number of decisions in which it ruled that a taking had occurred, even though no land was actually condemned. In two cases, *Nollan v. California Coastal Commission*, 483 U.S. 825 (1987), and *Dolan v. City of Tigard*, 512 U.S. 374 (1994), the Court ruled that the government had gone too far when it required owners to give the public a limited right to use their property in exchange for permission to build on it. In *Lucas v. South Carolina Coastal Council*, 505 U.S. 1003 (1992), it ruled that building restrictions that barred an owner from building homes on his property rendered it worthless.

Planning, Zoning, and Local Land-use Restrictions

From the time humans began to form communities, disputes have arisen when one person's use of property has interfered with the rights of property owners. In England, from which the United States inherited its legal system, those disputes were resolved by courts that applied *common law*, a collection of legal principles laid down by judges over the centuries.

English courts recognized the right to sue for *trespass*, the physical invasion of someone else's property, and for *private nuisance*, "a nontrespassory invasion of another's interest in the private use and enjoyment of land."[7] They also recognized the government's authority to put a stop to a *public nuisance*, "an unreasonable interference with a right common to the general public,"[8] such as maintaining a home where illegal drugs are sold.

Governments not only reacted to uses of land that harmed the public, but also passed laws designed to prevent harmful uses in the first place. The best-known land-use restrictions are zoning ordinances that dictate what can be built and where. They affect millions of Americans who live in cities and suburbs and are a fact of life in most communities. They were widely adopted in the early twentieth century after the Supreme Court concluded, in *Village of Euclid, Ohio v. Ambler Realty Company*, 272 U.S. 365 (1926), that a local zoning ordinance did not deprive property owners of due process of law.

Despite the *Euclid* decision, zoning ordinances have been challenged in court. Opponents argued that ordinances in some communities "zone out" people who are considered undesirable, such as the poor, members of minority groups, and the mentally impaired. A legal challenge to "exclusionary zoning" succeeded in *Southern Burlington County N.A.A.C.P. v. Township of Mount Laurel*, 67 N.J. 151, 336 A.2d 713 (N.J. Sup. Ct. 1975). In that case, the Supreme Court of New Jersey ruled that a community's zoning restrictions made it impossible for low- and middle-income families to live there. Critics

Condemnation Powers Reaffirmed: *Hawaii Housing Authority v. Midkiff*

The original Polynesian settlers of the Hawaiian Islands developed an economy based on feudalism. Under that system, an island high chief, the *ali'i nui*, controlled the land and assigned it for development to certain subchiefs. The subchiefs then reassigned the land to other, lower-ranking chiefs, who administered the land and governed the farmers and other tenants who worked on it. All land was held at the will of the *ali'i nui* and eventually had to be returned to his trust. There was no private ownership of land as known in contemporary American society.

Beginning in the early nineteenth century, Hawaiian leaders and American settlers repeatedly tried to break up the concentration of Hawaii's land, but they made little progress. Even after Hawaii became a state, the problem persisted. One factor that perpetuated concentration was the federal tax code: An owner who sold his property faced a huge tax bill because it was worth far more than he originally paid for it.

In 1967, the federal and state government owned about half of Hawaii's land and a handful of individuals owned almost all the rest. Lopsided land ownership drove up real estate prices and forced many Hawaiians to rent, rather than own, their homes. State lawmakers responded by passing the Land Reform Act, which allowed tenants to ask the Hawaii Housing Authority to condemn the property that they rented. If enough tenants made requests, the Housing Authority would begin condemnation proceedings.

Faced with condemnation, Frank Midkiff and two other landowners filed suit to stop the Housing Authority from taking their land. They argued that the Land Reform Act was unconstitutional because it authorized the taking of property from one private individual and transferring it to another. A federal appeals court agreed with them. The Housing Authority appealed to the United States Supreme

of zoning also argue that ordinances are not enforced even-handedly and that some restrictions unfairly burden a small group of property owners. Some property-rights advocates go even further and argue that most zoning restrictions are actually takings.

Court, which, in *Hawaii Housing Authority v. Midkiff*, 467 U.S. 229 (1984), unanimously ruled in its favor. Justice Sandra Day O'Connor wrote the Court's opinion.

Justice O'Connor concluded that the Land Reform Act did not violate the Public Use Clause. The starting point for her analysis was *Berman v. Parker*, which broadly defined the government's condemnation power. She went on to write, "The 'public use' requirement is thus coterminous with the scope of a sovereign's police powers." She added that the Court would not substitute its judgment for that of lawmakers as to what was a public use unless that use was "palpably without reasonable foundation."

Justice O'Connor concluded that Hawaii lawmakers had the authority to enact land-reform legislation. She pointed out that they, like the settlers of the 13 original colonies, had attempted "to reduce the perceived social and economic evils of a land oligopoly traceable to their monarchs" and went on to observe that "regulating oligopoly and the evils associated with it is a classic exercise of a State's police powers." She next found that the means that Hawaii's legislature had chosen to break up the oligopoly were not irrational.

Justice O'Connor next concluded that the Court had long ago rejected a literal requirement that condemned property be put to *use* for the general public. She wrote, "The Act advances its purposes without the State's taking actual possession of the land. In such cases, government does not itself have to use property to legitimate the taking; it is only the taking's purpose, and not its mechanics, that must pass scrutiny under the Public Use Clause."

Author Steven Greenhut, who believes that government has abused condemnation, contended that the Land Reform Act was not only unconstitutional but unnecessary: "It's unfortunate, then, that a problem exacerbated by the government couldn't be fixed with some tax exemptions and a sell-off of many parcels of government-owned land."[*]

[*]Steven Greenhut, *Abuse of Power: How the Government Misuses Eminent Domain*. Santa Ana, Calif.: Seven Locks Press, 2004, p. 104.

The Modern Property-rights Movement

The *Kelo* decision provoked heated debate, but a movement to defend property rights had been underway for many years. Now, as in pioneer days, many Americans distrust the federal government. That sentiment motivated the "Sagebrush Rebellion" of the 1970s, in which Western ranchers, miners, and other property owners formed coalitions to oppose the federal regulation of land in that region. Landowners also protested a variety of federal environmental laws that restricted mining, logging, and other activities that might pollute the air and water, upset a fragile ecosystem, or damage the habitats of endangered plants and animals. Although those restrictions reduced the value of the land, the government offered the owners no compensation.

The property-rights movement won a number of victories after Ronald Reagan was elected president in 1980. Reagan appointed westerners who supported property rights to his cabinet and named conservative Supreme Court justices who later handed down pro-landowner decisions such as *Nollan*, *Lucas*, and *Dolan*. Nevertheless, property-rights advocates believe that the scope of federal regulation has become more intrusive, especially in the area of environmental protection. They also complain that courts and legislatures have not done enough to protect landowners from regulatory takings. Congress has considered, but has not passed, legislation that would compensate landowners for the loss of value that results from federal regulation. At the state level, Oregon voters approved a broad regulatory-taking measure in 2004 and Arizona voters approved a similar measure in 2006. Meanwhile, property-rights advocates, such as the Institute for Justice, which represented Susette Kelo, continue their fight to scale back the government's power to condemn property. Despite their efforts, however, *Kelo* remains the law of the land.

What This Book Covers

"Property rights" is a broad topic. In fact, most law students spend two semesters studying property law. There are many forms of property, and this book focuses on *real property*, the land and structures that are attached to it. There are two reasons: First, the most bitter property-rights debates involve the use of land. Second, for much of history, real estate was the most widespread and important form of wealth and for that reason it has enjoyed special legal status.

This book also focuses on three major issues: eminent domain, such as the condemnation in *Kelo*; regulatory takings, especially the impact of federal environmental laws; and state and local land-use restrictions, such as zoning. All three issues involve a conflict between the same basic values: the individual rights of the property owner versus the interests of the community as a whole. Those values are fundamental to a variety of other land-use controversies that range from historic preservation to laws against smoking in restaurants.

Summary

The *Kelo* case, in which the Supreme Court ruled that government has broad powers to condemn property, provoked intense controversy. Critics maintain that the Court misread the Constitution and encouraged abusive condemnations. The fight over property rights is not limited to condemnation, however. Property-rights advocates also oppose a wide range of regulations that do not involve physical taking but nevertheless deprive owners of the full use of their property. Those regulations include federal environmental laws and local zoning and land-use restrictions. Because those laws diminish the value of property, advocates urge that they be treated as takings and that the affected owners receive compensation.

The Government Abuses Condemnation

The Takings Clause of the Constitution reflects the Framers' belief in the rule of law. As Professor Peter Hoffer of the University of Georgia explained, "Law is to be general, equally applied, feasible, predictable, stable, and clear to all. Lawmaking must be a public enterprise, blind to special interests and powerful individuals, rational, and accessible."[9]

Property-rights advocates maintain that the *Kelo* decision stood the rule of law on its head. They accuse the Supreme Court of having ignored the Framers' intent by adopting an almost limitless definition of "public purpose" and by allowing property rights to be swept aside for economic reasons. A quarter-century earlier, Justice James Ryan warned in his dissent in *Poletown* "how easily government, in all of its branches, caught up in the frenzy of perceived economic crisis, can disregard the rights of the few in allegiance to the always disastrous philosophy that the end justifies the means."[10]

Property rights are important civil rights.

Property rights were of paramount importance to those who founded this country. The Declaration of Independence stated that "all men are created equal, that they are endowed by their Creator with certain unalienable Rights, that among these are Life, Liberty and the pursuit of Happiness."[11] Many historians believe that private property rights were at the heart of the "pursuit of happiness." They add that the Takings Clause, along with several other provisions of the Bill of Rights, was aimed at protecting a citizen's home against government intrusion.

It has also been argued that property rights are an indispensable safeguard of political rights. Professor and author Jay Feinman explained:

> The ability to own property and thereby to establish a means of independence from others . . . makes it possible for the property owner to assert political independence. Sometimes it is said that property is a precondition of democracy, because property enables a citizen to speak freely and participate in public affairs without concern that political participation will undermine one's economic well-being.[12]

Nevertheless, many believe that courts no longer give property rights the respect they deserve. In a 1994 takings case, Chief Justice William Rehnquist wrote, "We see no reason why the Takings Clause of the Fifth Amendment, as much a part of the Bill of Rights as the First Amendment or Fourth Amendment, should be relegated to the status of a poor relation."[13]

Americans recognized the injustice of *Kelo*, and state lawmakers have responded to public opinion. According to the Institute for Justice, a substantial majority of states have placed restrictions on economic-development condemnations since *Kelo* was handed down.

The Court ignores the public use requirement.

Justice Sandra Day O'Connor argued that New London's redevelopment plan violated a centuries-old legal principle that the government may not take property from private party A and then give

FROM THE BENCH

What the *Kelo* Dissenters Wrote

There were two dissenting opinions in *Kelo*. The first, written by Justice Sandra Day O'Connor, argued that the majority had expanded the government's condemnation power beyond what the Takings Clause permitted. In her view, economic-development condemnations were contrary to more than 200 years of Supreme Court precedent. She argued:

> To reason, as the Court does, that the incidental public benefits resulting from the subsequent ordinary use of private property render economic development takings "for public use" is to wash out any distinction between private and public use of property—and thereby effectively to delete the words "for public use" from the Takings Clause of the Fifth Amendment.

Justice O'Connor maintained that the public-use requirement barred the government from condemning a person's property "for the benefit of another private person." A road, a publicly owned hospital, or a military base certainly qualified as a public use, and so did a railroad, a public utility, or a stadium, because those facilities would be available to the public. That, however, was not true of the redevelopment project proposed by New London. She added that the government "cannot take [existing owners'] property for the private use of other owners simply because the new owners may make more productive use of the property."

Justice O'Connor accused the majority of having misread both *Berman v. Parker* and *Hawaii Housing Authority v. Midkiff*. She explained:

> In both those cases, the extraordinary, precondemnation use of the targeted property inflicted affirmative harm on society—in *Berman* through blight resulting from extreme poverty and in *Midkiff* through oligopoly resulting from extreme wealth. And in both cases, the relevant legislative body had found that eliminating the existing property use was necessary to remedy the harm. Thus a public purpose was realized when the harmful use was eliminated.

it to private party B. Critics insist that the government routinely engages in such takings and that *Kelo* was not an exceptional case.

Critics allege that this has happened because the Supreme Court's "hands-off" approach has encouraged public officials

In this case, however, New London never proved that the homes targeted for condemnation were harmful.

Justice O'Connor argued that, under the majority's logic, there were virtually no limits to the condemnation power: "The trouble with economic development takings is that private benefit and incidental public benefit are, by definition, merged and mutually reinforcing. In this case, for example, any boon for Pfizer or the plan's developer is difficult to disaggregate from the promised public gains in taxes and jobs."

Finally, Justice O'Connor responded to the majority's suggestion that property-rights advocates turn to state legislatures and courts for help: "States play many important functions in our system of dual sovereignty, but compensating for our refusal to enforce properly the Federal Constitution (and a provision meant to curtail state action, no less) is not among them."

The second dissent, written by Justice Clarence Thomas, was more sweeping. Justice Thomas began by trying to determine what the Takings Clause meant at the time it was drafted. He concluded that the term "public use," as used by the Framers, "means that either the government or its citizens as a whole must actually 'employ' the taken property"—something that would not happen in this case.

Justice Thomas suggested that both *Berman* and *Midkiff*—which Justice O'Connor had approved of—were wrongly decided because the Court substituted "public purpose" for "public use" and then compounded the error by wrongly deferring to legislative judgments of what a valid "public purpose" was. He added that, in *Berman* and *Midkiff*, the Court wrongly equated the eminent domain power with the police power. He insisted that the condemnation power was narrower and cited the example of a public nuisance to prove his point: When the government exercised its police power to end a nuisance, it was not obligated to compensate the owner for damage to his or her property.

Finally, Justice Thomas argued that just compensation did not cover the subjective value of the condemned property or the indignity that resulted from being forced to give up one's home. He added that, over the years, members of minority groups were disproportionately targeted by exercises of the condemnation power.

to push the definition of "public use" to its limit and exercise condemnation powers that the Framers never intended. Justice Clarence Thomas, a dissenter in *Kelo*, argued that the Court never should have deferred to local officials in condemnation cases. He wrote,

> It is most implausible that the Framers intended to defer to legislatures as to what satisfies the Public Use Clause, uniquely among all the express provisions of the Bill of Rights. We would not defer to a legislature's determination of the various circumstances that establish, for example, when a search of a home would be reasonable.[14]

Justice Thomas also argued that the Court should enforce the public-use requirement as it was written. He wrote, "The government may take property only if it actually uses or gives the public a legal right to use the property."[15] In his *Poletown* dissent, Justice James Ryan offered his interpretation of "public use": property could be transferred from one private owner to another only under one of the following conditions: "1) *public* necessity of the extreme sort, 2) continuing accountability to the *public*, and 3) selection of land according to facts of independent *public* significance [emphasis original]."[16] He concluded that none of those conditions existed in *Poletown*. The same can be said of the condemnations in *Kelo*.

Condemnation serves special interests.

Scott Bullock, the lawyer who represented Susette Kelo, argued that eminent domain has powerful friends:

> Indeed, about the only people who support the abusive practices are those who stand to benefit from it: local political officials, including big city mayors such as New York's Michael Bloomberg; and planners and developers. What these beneficiaries lack in numbers, however, they more than make up for in political muscle.[17]

In his book *Abuse of Power*, Steven Greenhut cited instances in which the government condemned property that belonged to

Susette Kelo talks to reporters outside the Supreme Court on February 22, 2005. She is accompanied by her attorney, Scott Bullock, who argued that the "only people who support the abusive practices are those who stand to benefit" from eminent domain.

homeowners and small businesses and turned it over to retailers, auto dealerships, and land developers.

Some believe that Justice O'Connor was right and that *Kelo* made the problem of condemnation abuse even worse. After *Kelo* was decided, the mayor of North Hills, New York, took steps to condemn a privately owned golf course so that it could be turned into an exclusive country club. Edward Herlihy, a lawyer who lived in that community, argued that the condemnation would serve no public purpose and, in any event, made no economic sense:

> If North Hills condemns [the course], the Constitution would require it to pay 'just compensation' for the value of

the property—which would be prohibitively expensive. The village would have to float a huge bond issue to raise that amount, and would have to increase property taxes significantly to pay for the bonds.[18]

Poletown Neighborhood Council v. City of Detroit

In early 1980, General Motors Corporation told the city of Detroit that it intended to close two auto plants that were located in the city. It offered to build a replacement plant if a suitable site could be found. The city eventually found a site, which included a close-knit ethnic neighborhood known as Poletown. Some of its residents refused to sell their homes to make way for the plant, and the city moved to condemn the homes.

An activist group that represented Poletown's residents sued to block the condemnations. It argued that using eminent domain to transfer property from one private owner to another violated the public-use requirement of the Michigan Constitution. The case quickly went up to the Supreme Court of Michigan which, in *Poletown Neighborhood Council v. City of Detroit*, 410 Mich. 616, 304 N.W.2d 455 (Mich. Sup. Ct. 1981), ruled that the condemnations were constitutional. The vote was 5 to 2.

The majority concluded that "public use" and "public purpose" were interchangeable and that those phrases were "protean," or capable of changing meaning. Following the United States Supreme Court's approach in *Berman v. Parker*, the justices refused to second-guess the city's conclusion that the new plant would generate jobs and tax revenue. The majority also concluded that the benefit to General Motors was "merely incidental" and that the public benefit was "so clear and significant" that it would not hesitate to approve the condemnation.

Justice James Ryan, one of two dissenters, criticized the majority for having put the case on a fast track, largely to meet a deadline imposed by General Motors, and for having made bad law "in allegiance to the always disastrous philosophy that the end justifies the means."

Until this decision, Justice Ryan argued, Michigan's courts had consistently drawn a distinction between "public use" and "public purpose" and, in addition, had given "little or no weight" to legislative determinations of whether a taking was for a public use. Because the majority ignored years of precedent, he wrote, "The state taking clause has now been placed on a spectrum that admits of no

Some of the costliest condemnation abuses have involved stadiums for professional sports teams. The city of Arlington, Texas, used its eminent domain power to clear land for a new ballpark for the Texas Rangers baseball club. It not only condemned land needed for the ballpark, but also seized surrounding land where

principles and therefore no limits." Justice Ryan also argued that the majority should not have followed *Berman* because that decision interpreted the Fifth Amendment's Takings Clause, not the Michigan Constitution.

Justice Ryan concluded that the government could condemn private property and transfer it to another private owner only if one of three criteria were present. The first criterion was "public necessity of the extreme sort," such as land in the path of a proposed railroad, because landowners who refused to sell could stop the railroad from operating. The second criterion was "continuing accountability to the public," for example, land that would be transferred to a utility that would operate under state regulation. The final criterion was selection of land according to "facts of independent public significance," such as a blighted structure that endangered public safety. In this case, Justice Ryan found that none of the criteria applied: Poletown was not the only possible location for a new plant; General Motors would be answerable to shareholders, not state regulators; and the site was selected for GM's benefit, not the public's. He added that "there may never be a clearer case than this of condemning land for a private corporation" and accused General Motors of having all but dictated the terms of the redevelopment plan to city officials.

The *Poletown* decision led to a wave of condemnations in the state. The September 14, 2003, *Detroit News* reported that Michigan had become "a national hotbed of eminent-domain cases" and that Detroit ranked first in the nation in condemnations. The debate over eminent domain came to a head shortly after that story appeared. A number of owners challenged the condemnation of their land to make way for a business and technology park. County officials argued that the park would revitalize a stagnant area, creating jobs and increasing tax revenue. The lawsuit reached the Supreme Court of Michigan which, in *County of Wayne v. Hathcock*, 471 Mich. 445, 684 N.W.2d 765 (Mich. Sup. Ct. 2004), followed the reasoning of Justice Ryan's dissent in *Poletown* and ruled unanimously that the condemnations violated the Michigan Constitution. In his majority opinion, Justice Robert Young described *Poletown* as "a radical departure from fundamental constitutional principles" and declared that decision overruled.

hotels, restaurants, and office buildings could be built, at a substantial profit to the Rangers's owners. According to Nicholas Kristof of the *New York Times*, the owners, not the city, were in charge of the condemnation effort:

> Confidential memos among the Rangers owners . . . paint a picture of the owners casting a proprietary eye over the area and then telling the city what land to seize. In one internal memo, for example, an owner referred to a privately owned parcel and told the other owners that it "sounds like another condemnation candidate—if you want to work the site into your master plan."[19]

Condemnation can also pit government officials against their own citizens. After Hurricane Katrina, New Orleans's redevelopment commission moved to condemn storm-damaged homes and businesses. Emily Chamlee-Wright and Daniel Rothschild of George Mason University accused the city of heavy-handed behavior: "Local government officials, armed with the public health code, eminent domain powers and a bevy of dubious legal techniques, aim to demolish buildings—and, some fear, strip titles from owners—in what are being euphemistically called 'forced buyouts.'"[20] They added that local land developers, who stood to profit from the condemnations, sat on the redevelopment commission.

Property owners receive inadequate compensation.

The Takings Clause requires the government to pay just compensation to those whose property is condemned. Critics argue, however, that the compensation owners actually receive rarely makes up for their economic losses. The Supreme Court has admitted as much. In a dispute that arose out of a condemnation that took place during World War II, the Court stated:

> No doubt all these elements [of damages] would be considered by an owner in determining whether, and at what price,

to sell. No doubt, therefore, if the owner is to be made whole for the loss consequent on the sovereign's seizure of his property, these elements should properly be considered. But the courts have generally held that they are not to be reckoned as part of the compensation for the [property rights] taken by the Government.[21]

Sixty years later, property owners continue to be short-changed. Steven Greenhut wrote, "Almost always, the government tries to lowball the property owner, in many cases offering a fraction of the property's value. The victim must hire an expensive lawyer to argue for the 'just compensation' the U.S. Constitution promises to eminent domain's victims."[22] He added that property owners often have to wage a long and expensive legal battle for compensation. Because the U.S. legal system requires parties to a lawsuit to pay their own legal fees, owners almost always lose money in condemnation cases. Businesses suffer additional losses because they generally get no compensation for being forced out of a prime location or having to move far away from their customers.

Just compensation also does not take into account the psychological damage of being displaced. As the Supreme Court of Ohio observed in a recent condemnation case, "For the individual property owner, the appropriation is not simply the seizure of a house. It is the taking of a home—the place where ancestors toiled, where families were raised, where memories were made."[23]

Condemnation does more harm than good.

In *Kelo*, the Supreme Court accepted New London's determination that the redevelopment project would benefit the public. The benefits that officials promise often fail to materialize, however. Charlotte Allen, a writer from Washington, D.C., makes her home in the area that was redeveloped by the project that the Court upheld in *Berman v. Parker*. She described the area as dominated by massive, featureless buildings, including a near-empty mall, with few small businesses and little vitality.

Allen maintained that what happened in southwest Washington is not unique: "Hundreds of smaller-scale eminent-domain-fueled redevelopment projects have followed relentlessly in cities across the country, including failed 'Renaissance' centers in Pittsburgh and Detroit."[24]

State Lawmakers Respond to *Kelo*-type Takings

The Institute for Justice, which represented Susette Kelo in her condemnation fight, has been monitoring state legislation aimed at outlawing or restricting *Kelo*-type takings. In October 2006, the institute reported that lawmakers in 31 states have enacted new restrictions on state and local eminent-domain power. That number grew in the 2006 elections, when voters in a number of states approved "anti-*Kelo*" measures. Some of the proposals that have become law since *Kelo* was decided include these:

- Tightening the definition of "blight" and limiting how long the government can rely on a study that found an area to be blighted (Pennsylvania) and requiring the government to prove by "clear and convincing evidence" that property is in fact blighted (Colorado).

- Requiring the government to give six months' notice before starting condemnation proceedings (Delaware).

- Imposing a 10-year waiting period on the transfer of condemned property to another private owner (Florida) and allowing the former owner the right to buy condemned property if the government attempts to transfer it to another private owner within seven years (South Dakota).

- Requiring the government to use a parcel-by-parcel approach in condemning blighted property rather than condemning an entire area as blighted (Kansas).

- Banning condemnations primarily for the purpose of enhancing tax revenue (Maine).

- Stripping redevelopment agencies of the power to condemn land (Utah).

Steven Greenhut described another failure, a huge redevelopment project that left North Hollywood, California, worse off
than it was before. That came as no surprise to him:

> Once an area is termed blighted and placed in a redevelop-
> ment area, everything stops. Property owners stop investing
> in their properties. Everyone waits for the government to
> spearhead the project. And the developers involved in the deal
> often take the taxpayers to the cleaners.[25]

Greenhut added that nearby areas that relied on market forces
rather than on government-led redevelopment fared better than
North Hollywood.

Opponents also point out that condemnation targets the
politically weak. Older neighborhoods populated by working-
class and ethnic families are especially at risk of being declared
"blighted" and leveled to make room for more profitable developments. In many parts of the country, the law defines "blight"
in such open-ended terms that it invites abuse. In Lakewood,
Ohio, for example, city officials took steps to declare a residential
neighborhood "blighted" and replace it with upscale condo-
miniums. Lakewood's definition of blight was so broad that, as
Greenhut observed, "Any house that didn't have three bedrooms,
two baths, a two-car attached garage and central air condition-
ing was blight. That encompassed 90 percent of the city's homes,
including the mayor's."[26]

Finally, in his dissenting opinion in *Kelo*, Justice Clarence
Thomas accused city planners of targeting minority-owned
property. He pointed out:

> Of all the families displaced by urban renewal from 1949
> through 1963, 63 percent of those whose race was known
> were nonwhite. . . . Public works projects in the 1950's and
> 1960's destroyed predominantly minority communities in
> St. Paul, Minnesota, and Baltimore, Maryland. . . . Over 97

percent of the individuals forcibly removed from their homes by the "slum-clearance" project upheld by this Court in *Berman* were black.[27]

Although cities have abandoned the massive slum-clearance projects that Justice Thomas referred to, critics believe that there still are racial overtones to the use of eminent domain.

Summary

Kelo resulted in a further expansion of eminent domain powers beyond the limits set out in the Takings Clause. Government officials, exercising those broad powers, often misclassify property as "blighted" or fail to put condemned property to a true public use. Instead, it is often turned over to wealthy businesses or developers to be used for projects that provide little or no benefit to the public. The compensation that is given to property owners rarely makes up for financial losses they suffer, let alone being uprooted from their homes. Condemnation is often used against citizens who lack political power, especially the poor and members of minority groups.

Condemnation Promotes the Public Welfare

The phrase "eminent domain" comes from the Latin *dominium eminens*, which means "transcendent sovereignty." Condemnation is a fundamental power of government, on a par with taxing and spending. As the Supreme Court of Ohio observed in a recent condemnation case:

> Wherever there is sovereignty, whether in the old world, where it is held in trust for the people by things called kings, or in this country where the people wear it upon their own shoulders, two great and fundamental rights exist: the right of eminent domain in all the people, and the right of private property in each. These great rights exist over and above, and independent of all human conventions, written and unwritten.[28]

Although the Framers of the Constitution placed limits on condemnation, they recognized that it was indispensable as a power of government.

The *Kelo* decision followed established principles of law.

Supporters of *Kelo* point out that it did not create new constitutional law. Instead, it followed the reasoning of *Berman v. Parker*, which upheld the use of condemnation to carry out a redevelopment project aimed at preventing future blight, and *Hawaii Housing Authority v. Midkiff*, which concluded that the power to condemn property was as broad as police power. *Midkiff* also recognized that state and local officials have broad authority to determine when condemnations advance the public welfare. As Sandra Day O'Connor wrote in that case,

> The Hawaii Legislature enacted its Land Reform Act not to benefit a particular class of identifiable individuals, but to attack certain perceived evils of concentrated property ownership in Hawaii—a legitimate public purpose. Use of the condemnation power to achieve this purpose is not irrational.[29]

Midkiff reinforced the Court's long-standing policy of broadly defining "public use." In *Fallbrook Irrigation District v. Bradley*, 164 U.S. 112 (1896), and several cases from the early twentieth century, the Supreme Court upheld the use of eminent domain for what could be termed "economic development" projects. As the Supreme Court of Ohio explained:

> By the end of the 19th century, the federal courts ... employed broad constructions of "public use" ... particularly when the taking expanded the economy or provided vital resources, as with mining operations or irrigation systems necessary for settlement and development of the western regions. . . [30]

The broader concept of public use set forth in these cases eventually dominated and became entrenched in early-twentieth-century eminent-domain jurisprudence.

In addition, federal courts traditionally refused to interfere with state and local government decisions relating to condemnation. As Justice John Paul Stevens wrote in *Kelo*:

> Our earliest cases in particular embodied a strong theme of federalism, emphasizing the "great respect" that we owe to state legislatures and state courts in discerning local public needs. . . . For more than a century, our public use jurisprudence has wisely eschewed rigid formulas and intrusive scrutiny in favor of affording legislatures broad latitude in determining what public needs justify the use of the takings power.[31]

From the time the Court decided *Berman* until *Kelo* was argued, federal appeals courts decided 31 cases in which the public-use requirement was an issue. They sided with the government in all but one, a case in which the taking did not meet Indiana's public-use requirement. The *Kelo* court continued that policy. It deferred to Connecticut lawmakers, who passed a law that detailed the benefits of economic-redevelopment projects, and to Connecticut's highest court, which heard arguments from both sides before voting, 4 to 3, to allow New London to go forward with the condemnations.

Economic development projects benefit the public.

Critics not only call *Kelo*-type condemnations unconstitutional but also suggest that encouraging economic development is not a legitimate function of government. Government officials, however, insist that development projects provide benefits that more than offset the occasional injustice to property owners such as Susette Kelo.

THE LETTER OF THE LAW

Connecticut's Justification for Economic Redevelopment

In *Kelo*, the Supreme Court accepted at face value the city of New London's conclusion that redeveloping its downtown would further a public purpose and that condemnation was a necessary means of carrying it out.

City officials carried out the redevelopment project under the authority of state laws that governed such projects. One provision, §8-124 of the General Statutes of Connecticut, set out the legislature's reasons why redevelopment is sometimes necessary:

> It is found and declared that there have existed and will continue to exist in the future in municipalities of the state substandard, insanitary, deteriorated, deteriorating, slum or blighted areas which constitute a serious and growing menace, injurious and inimical to the public health, safety, morals and welfare of the residents of the state; that the existence of such areas contributes substantially and increasingly to the spread of disease and crime, necessitating excessive and disproportionate expenditures of public funds for the preservation of the public health and safety, for crime prevention... and the treatment of juvenile delinquency and for the maintenance of adequate police, fire and accident protection and other public services and facilities, and the existence of such areas constitutes an economic and social liability, substantially impairs or arrests the sound growth of municipalities, and retards the provision of housing accommodation; that this menace is beyond remedy and control solely by regulatory process in the exercise of the police power and cannot be dealt with effectively by the ordinary operations of private enterprise without the aids herein provided; that the acquisition of property for the purpose of eliminating substandard ... or blighted conditions thereon or preventing recurrence of such conditions in the area, the removal of structures and improvement of sites, the disposition of the property for redevelopment incidental to the foregoing, the exercise of powers by municipalities acting through agencies known as redevelopment agencies as herein provided, and any assistance which may be given by any public body in connection therewith, are public uses and purposes for which public money may be expended and the power of eminent domain exercised; and that the necessity in the public interest for the provisions of this chapter is hereby declared as a matter of legislative determination.

The American Planning Association maintains that projects such as New London's redevelopment reflect a "smart growth" strategy: refurbishing older communities that already have infrastructure such as roads and power lines rather than spending money to build new ones. Existing cities also have other assets, such as waterfront land and buildings with historic significance. Government action is needed to unlock their value. The association explained that redevelopment is appropriate for

> an area that was developed at some time in the past but presently suffers from real or perceived physical deficiencies such as blight or environmental contamination or is developed for uses that have become obsolete or inappropriate as a result of changing social or market conditions.[32]

Planners also contend that redeveloping existing communities curbs suburban sprawl, the negative effects of which include pollution, destruction of wildlife habitat, and the decline of older communities that leads to even more sprawl.

Critics of economic development attack condemnation, but condemnation is just one of a variety of tools that are used to refurbish communities. The American Planning Association cites a number of other methods, which include "direct public investment, capital improvements, enhanced public services, technical assistance, promotion, tax benefits, and rezoning."[33]

One of critics' most vehement objections to economic-development projects is that condemned property is turned over to private developers. The planning community, however, believes that partnerships between the government and private businesses best serve the public interest. As the American Planning Association explained:

> Many communities have observed through experience that the private sector is most often more nimble, more capable of making appropriate risk/reward decisions, and, in general, more effective at being developers or redevelopers than is the

Houses in North Philadelphia stand abandoned in the above photograph from 2002. In many cities across the country, urban blight has taken hold, and the only way to eliminate it is to condemn the buildings so that the government may take over the land.

public sector. At the same time, use of the authority and power of the public to act in the best interest of the community may be, in some circumstances, the only means by which development or redevelopment may overcome market forces in a way that best promotes the larger public interest.[34]

Sometimes there is no alternative to condemnation.

Although government officials consider condemnation a last resort, there are situations in which no alternative exists. Perhaps the best-known situation is the "holdout" property owner. In Fitzgerald, Georgia, for example, the city condemned abandoned or dilapidated homes whose owners refused to sell. The National

League of Cities commented that "the power of condemnation is critical in this case, because one absentee landlord cannot condemn an entire neighborhood to live with blight."[35]

Other unusual circumstances may force the government to use its eminent domain power. Louisville officials moved to condemn a railroad bridge over the Ohio River after the bridge's owners demanded what the city thought was an unreasonable amount of compensation. The bridge stood in the way of completing a waterfront development project. Another example was a blighted building in Valdosta, Georgia. The out-of-state owner of a one-third interest in the building refused to sell, even at fair market value. The city used eminent domain as a last resort "to gain ownership of it for the purpose of eliminating a blight, to assist neighboring properties who had made sizeable investments in their property only to have a vacant, blighted structure next to them and to try to get this building back on the tax rolls as a contributing piece of property."[36]

Likewise, condemnation can be an essential tool in carrying out redevelopment projects. The National League of Cities cited the example of Newport, Kentucky, which recently refurbished its aging downtown:

> In 1996 when the process began, the area was blighted with vacant buildings spread over 10 acres that belonged to more than 70 different property owners. In 1998, the city began in earnest to acquire the various properties using eminent domain.
>
> Today that blighted area is has been transformed to a shopping and entertainment complex that attracts more than three million visitors a year.[37]

The law already restricts condemnations.

Property-rights advocates insist that courts must curb the abuse of eminent domain. There already exists an array of legal checks on condemnation, however. Procedural requirements, such as having the property appraised beforehand or allowing a jury to decide how much compensation is "just," make condemnation so expensive and time-consuming that government officials try to avoid it when possible. As a result, condemnation is generally reserved for property that an owner cannot or will not sell.

Local officials, who have to face voters, are also mindful of the political ramifications of condemnation. For that reason, they frequently offer financial incentives to homeowners who

THE LETTER OF THE LAW

Arizona's Takings Clause

The majority in *Kelo* reaffirmed the Supreme Court's long-standing policy of deferring to state and local officials' determination of what is a "public use" in condemnation cases. It also pointed out that states can—and often do—impose more stringent limits on the condemnation power.

Arizona is one such state. Article 2, §17, of the Arizona Constitution provides:

Private property shall not be taken for private use, except for private ways of necessity, and for drains, flumes, or ditches, on or across the lands of others for mining, agricultural, domestic, or sanitary purposes. No private property shall be taken or damaged for public or private use without just compensation having first been made, paid into court for the owner, secured by bond as may be fixed by the court, or paid into the state treasury for the owner on such terms and conditions as the legislature may provide, and no right of way shall be appropriated to the use of any corporation other than municipal, until full compensation therefore be first made in money, or ascertained and paid into court for the owner, irrespective of any benefit from any improvement proposed by such corporation, *which compensation shall be ascertained by a jury*, unless a jury be waived as in other civil cases in courts of record, in the manner prescribed by law. Whenever an attempt is made to take private property for a use alleged to be public, *the question whether the contemplated use be really public shall be a judicial question*, and determined as such without regard to any legislative assertion that the use is public (emphasis added).

are forced to leave. Eddie Perez, the mayor of Hartford, Connecticut, told a committee of the United States Senate:

> Hartford's use of eminent domain in the past has underscored the City's appreciation for those individuals affected so that the Hartford community can prosper. Frequently, these individuals are not only compensated for their property at prices well above market value, but receive significant and lengthy additional government funding for their relocation.[38]

Supporters argue that a court-imposed limit on eminent domain is too drastic a remedy. The National League of Cities admits that condemnation law is not perfect but insists that legislators can reform those laws without the courts doing it for them. One reform, aimed at helping displaced homeowners such as Susette Kelo, is to offer compensation for "subjective damage." The league explained,

> Subjective value has many sources. Owners may have made modifications to the property to suit their individual needs and preferences; they may treasure friendships they have formed in the neighborhood; they may simply enjoy the security that comes from being in familiar surroundings. These values are ignored under the fair market value test.[39]

Another reform suggested by the National League of Cities is compensation for "consequential damages," such as a business' lost goodwill as a consequence of being forced to move.

Supporters of condemnation accuse property-rights forces of reading the Takings Clause too literally and warn that such a reading would leave that clause "frozen in time." As the American Planning Association explained:

> The Fifth Amendment has not been amended since it was adopted in 1791. If only those projects recognized as proper objects of eminent domain in 1791 were deemed permissible,

huge swathes of settled eminent domain law would now have to be repudiated as unconstitutional. If we decide that 1868, when the Fourteenth Amendment was adopted, is the appropriate reference point, then the effect would be only slightly less [drastic]. Takings for public utility lines, pipelines, water reclamation projects, and urban renewal were all unrecognized as of 1868.[40]

THE LETTER OF THE LAW

What Is Blight?

Despite the legislative reaction to *Kelo*, officials in some states still have wide power to condemn property to redevelop neighborhoods because the law defines "blight" broadly and state courts defer to officials' determination that blight exists.

Title 11, Section 38-101(8) of the Oklahoma Statutes is an example of a broad definition of a "blighted area":

> "Blighted area" shall mean an area in which there are properties, buildings, or improvements, whether occupied or vacant, whether residential or nonresidential, which by reason of dilapidation, deterioration, age or obsolescence, inadequate provision for ventilation, light, air, sanitation or open spaces; population overcrowding; improper subdivision or obsolete platting of land, inadequate parcel size; arrested economic development; improper street layout in terms of existing or projected traffic needs, traffic congestion or lack of parking or terminal facilities needed for existing or proposed land uses in the area, predominance of defective or inadequate street layouts; faulty lot layout in relation to size, adequacy, accessibility or usefulness; insanitary or unsafe conditions, deterioration of site or other improvements; diversity of ownership, tax or special assessment delinquency exceeding the fair value of the land; defective or unusual conditions of title; any one or combination of such conditions which substantially impair or arrest the sound growth of municipalities, or constitutes an economic or social liability, or which endangers life or property by fire or other causes, or is conducive to ill health, transmission of disease, mortality, juvenile delinquency, or crime and by reason thereof, is detrimental to the public health, safety, morals or welfare.

It has also been argued that a literal interpretation of the Takings Clause could be harmful to older communities. Anthony Williams, mayor of Washington, D.C., warned what would happen if economic-development condemnations were found unconstitutional: "In the face of potential federal budget cuts of dramatic proportions and the inability to impose limitless taxes, how will they be able to attract private investment in areas where weeds and boarded-up buildings may be the norm?"[41]

Claims of condemnation abuse are exaggerated.
Public officials believe that the property-rights movement has painted a misleading picture of condemnation. As Hartford's Mayor Perez explained,

> The press has incorrectly reported that the *Kelo* decision greatly expands local government authority giving city leaders permission to take homes without warning and without adequate compensation. This feeds the public's fears that bulldozers, which allegedly stand at Grandma's gate, engines roaring, are heading next for their homes.[42]

In practice, eminent domain is generally reserved for extraordinary cases and accounts for only a small fraction of land that is needed for redevelopment projects. In New London, for example, only 2 percent of the land needed for redevelopment was acquired by condemnation.

Opponents of condemnation focus on its misuse and disregard its benefits. Bart Peterson, the mayor of Indianapolis, Indiana, told a subcommittee of the United States Senate about an eminent domain success story in his city:

> The area, now called Fall Creek Place, was blighted and known for its violence and drugs. The private sector was unable to change these conditions, as it could not do anything about the abandoned homes and poorly maintained

vacant lots. The city acquired 250 properties. Of those, 28 were eminent domain cases. We did not use eminent domain against any property owner's will, but only when the property owners could not be located. Today Fall Creek Place is a beautiful mixed-income neighborhood with homeowners of all backgrounds, including a majority of low-income residents, and 71 percent that are first-time homeowners.[43]

Other success stories include Lincoln Center in New York, Baltimore's Inner Harbor, and Boston's Convention and Exhibition Center.

Summary

The *Kelo* decision did not create new law; instead, it followed well-established legal principles. For more than a century, the Supreme Court has read the Takings Clause's public-use requirement broadly and refused to second-guess condemnation decisions made by state and local officials. Condemning property is only one of a variety of tools that communities use to revitalize themselves. Although government officials consider condemnation a last resort, they must sometimes use it in order to acquire needed land. They argue that court-imposed restrictions on eminent domain are unnecessary.

Land-use Restrictions Are Unjust to Property Owners

I n July 2006, a lawsuit filed under the federal Endangered Species Act held up work on a $320 million irrigation project in Arkansas. In that case, a federal judge concluded that the ivory-billed woodpecker might be living on the land in question and ordered the Army Corps of Engineers to come forward with evidence that the project would not jeopardize the bird.

What made this case unusual is that no one knows for certain whether the ivory-billed woodpecker still exists. The last confirmed sighting in North America occurred in 1944, and scientists thought that the species was extinct until 2004, when a kayaker claimed to have found one in the area. There is no conclusive evidence confirming that finding, however.

To property-rights advocates, cases such as this demonstrate that land-use restrictions, especially those intended to protect the environment, impose unreasonable costs on unlucky landowners.

Many regulations are takings without compensation.

Many regulations reduce the value of property so significantly that property-rights advocates argue that the regulations are in fact takings for which the affected owners should be compensated. In his dissent in *Penn Central Transportation Company v. New York City*, Justice William Rehnquist expressed his view that a New York City ordinance that restricted development of historic landmarks was what some critics call a "taking on the cheap." He wrote:

> The city of New York is in a precarious financial state, and some may believe that the costs of landmark preservation will be more easily borne by corporations such as Penn Central than the overburdened individual taxpayers of New York. But these concerns do not allow us to ignore past precedents construing the Eminent Domain Clause to the end that the desire to improve the public condition is, indeed, achieved by a shorter cut than the constitutional way of paying for the change.[44]

The practice of regulating land use without compensating the owner is popular with voters because they receive the benefits of regulation for free. Professor Robert Bruegmann of the University of Illinois at Chicago cited the example of Oregon's statewide land-use restrictions. Those restrictions appealed to state residents "because of a perception that by simply mandating the growth boundary, rather than buying development rights the way the British did, citizens can secure open space and other public benefits without paying for them."[45]

Roger Pilon, who is now a scholar at the Cato Institute in Washington, attempted to draw the line between regulations and takings:

> "When is the state required to compensate those it regulates?"—can be answered as follows. First, when the activity

prohibited is a rights violating activity, no compensation is required, for the activity is illegitimate to begin with. Second, when the activity is legitimate, the state has no right to prohibit it. But, third, when the state does prohibit such an activity anyway, in order to achieve some "public good," then it is required to compensate those from whom the rightful activity was taken, every bit as much as in eminent domain.[46]

Under that standard, many land-use regulations fall into the category of takings, but the owners do not receive a penny in compensation. In other words, their property has been stolen.

Because of the growing trend toward regulation without compensation, some have called property rights "the nation's newest civil-rights issue." Nancie Marzulla, who founded Defenders of Property Rights, views regulation as part of a larger assault on ownership rights:

> Today, property rights has become the line drawn in the sand between tyranny and liberty. As a result, the American public is coming to realize that the environmental ethic is based less on environmental protection and more on the false pretense that people should have only limited rights to own and use their property, and only when it is deemed acceptable to government regulators.[47]

Some activists even compare the actions of government regulators to those of the English kings and view property-rights legislation as a modern-day Magna Carta.

Government regulators make bad decisions.

Environmental laws are often enforced by career civil servants rather than by elected officials. They get to exercise broad authority, yet do not have to face voters. Furthermore, because they are salaried government employees rather than business

owners, they are not held accountable for the economic consequences of their actions. Nancie Marzulla explained, "A property
owner who blights his or her land destroys his or her own estate
and that of his or her heirs. A bureaucrat who blights 'public'
land bears no cost whatsoever. When land belongs to everyone,
it actually belongs to no one."[48]

When Regulation "Goes Too Far": *Pennsylvania Coal Company v. Mahon*

During the 1920s, a conservative United States Supreme Court struck down a
number of economic regulations as violations of "substantive due process." Under
this open-ended legal doctrine, judges invalidated laws that violated their notion
of "liberty."

One notable substantive due process decision was *Pennsylvania Coal Company v. Mahon*, 260 U.S. 393 (1922). That case arose after Pennsylvania lawmakers
banned coal mining that would cause subsidence—the lowering of Earth's surface—underneath homes and other structures. At the time the law took effect,
the Pennsylvania Coal Company owned the rights to mine coal underneath land
whose surface rights belonged to others.

The coal company challenged the law in court, arguing that the ban on mining
would extinguish its contract and property rights and thus deny it due process of
law. The Supreme Court ruled in the coal company's favor.

Justice Oliver Wendell Holmes wrote the majority opinion. He conceded that
government "hardly could go on" if every regulation that diminished property
values was found unconstitutional and noted that property values "are enjoyed
under an implied limitation and must yield to the police power." Justice Holmes
went on to write, however, that "while property may be regulated to a certain
extent, if regulation goes too far it will be recognized as a taking." In this case,
Justice Holmes concluded that the coal company had suffered a taking because
"to make it commercially impracticable to mine certain coal has very nearly the
same effect for constitutional purposes as appropriating or destroying it." Justice
Holmes also cautioned against the practice of seizing property without paying
compensation: "We are in danger of forgetting that a strong public desire to

James Rinehart and Jeffrey Pompe, professors at Francis Marion University, suggested that government regulators tend to make decisions that defy economic sense:

If the government has to pay for things which it has previously gotten for free, it may start to think about whether

improve the public condition is not enough to warrant achieving the desire by a shorter cut than the constitutional way of paying for the change."

Justice Louis Brandeis dissented. He maintained that preventing subsidence was a valid exercise of the police power. He added that an owner may not use land to create a public nuisance and that "uses, once harmless, may, owing to changed conditions, seriously threaten the public welfare." Justice Brandeis also described the Pennsylvania law as one that prevented a "noxious use" of property. Regarding the scope of the police power in general, Justice Brandeis wrote:

Restriction upon use does not become inappropriate as a means, merely because it deprives the owner of the only use to which the property can then be profitably put.... Nor is a restriction imposed through exercise of the police power inappropriate as a means, merely because the same end might be effected through exercise of the power of eminent domain, or otherwise at public expense.

Although the law extinguished the coal company's contract rights, Justice Brandeis maintained that those rights did not supersede the police power. He also stated that the power to protect the public welfare could not be bargained away.

By 1937, the Court's membership had changed. The new justices stopped using substantive due process to invalidate economic regulation such as the mining law that was challenged in *Pennsylvania Coal*. Instead, they adopted a "rational basis" test, a very low level of scrutiny, for economic regulation. Substantive due process has not disappeared entirely at the federal level, but it is for the most part limited to legal restrictions on marriage, raising children, and other intimate personal decisions. The best-known substantive due process decision of the modern Supreme Court is *Roe v. Wade*, 410 U.S. 113 (1973), which struck down most state restrictions on abortion.

these things are worth the cost. Is it really worth it to preserve wetlands? Is it really worth it to preserve beaches or species or historical things if we have to pay for them?[49]

Supporters of property rights hold up *Lucas v. South Carolina Coastal Council* as an example of bad decision making by regulators. The state settled David Lucas's lawsuit against it by agreeing to buy his lots. Later, it decided to resell them to another developer but received only about half of what it

Land-Use Restriction Ruled a Taking: *Lucas v. South Carolina Coastal Council*

In 1986, David Lucas bought two lots on the Isle of Palms, South Carolina. Two years later, the South Carolina Coastal Council, acting under the authority of a state law that regulated development along the seashore, ruled that Lucas's lots were part of a "critical area" that could not be built on. Lucas then filed suit. He argued that the council's action had made his property worthless and thus amounted to a taking.

The Supreme Court of South Carolina concluded that no taking had occurred because the state's coastal-zone regulations were police power regulations aimed at preventing serious harm to the public. The United States Supreme Court, which had begun to revisit the issue of regulatory takings, decided to hear Lucas's appeal. In *Lucas v. South Carolina Coastal Council*, 505 U.S. 1003 (1992), six of the nine justices ruled in his favor. Justice Antonin Scalia wrote the majority opinion.

Justice Scalia observed that earlier Court decisions had recognized two forms of regulation that amounted to takings: one that results in a physical invasion of a person's land and one that "denies all economically beneficial or productive use of land." He concluded that this case fell into the second category and wrote that "when the owner of real property has been called upon to sacrifice all economically beneficial uses in the name of the common good, that is, to leave his property economically idle, he has suffered a taking." Justice Scalia then announced a two-part rule for determining when a regulatory taking had occurred: first, the regulation denies *all* economically productive or beneficial use of land, and sec-

had paid for them. Professors Rinehart and Pompe called the final disposition of the lots "the most significant aspect" of the *Lucas* case. They explained,

> It points up the ease with which government is willing to impose restrictions on property owners when the cost is borne by the owner, but the reluctance to subject the state to the same restriction when the cost burden falls on a government agency budget.[50]

---

ond, the owner's intended use of his land would not be a nuisance and would not violate some other principle of property law.

Justice Harry Blackmun dissented. He accused the majority of having overturned a long line of Supreme Court decisions that found land-use regulations constitutional, even when they deprived the owner of most of the value of his land. Justice Blackmun added that the majority's new rule was so uncertain that it could invite lawsuits that challenged other restrictions on land use. He also maintained that Lucas's lots had not been "taken" because they still had some value. For example, they could be used for recreational purposes or sold to a neighbor as a buffer. Justice John Paul Stevens, another dissenter, called the new rule "wholly arbitrary" because, under it, an owner whose land lost 95 percent of its value would recover nothing but an owner whose land lost 100 percent of its value would receive full compensation. He argued that the rule would encourage clever lawyers to create new forms of property—such as the right to build a multifamily home on a specific lot—and allow the owner to argue that a regulation barring him from building such a home was a taking. Justice Stevens also warned that the rule could prevent the government from deciding in the future that currently-lawful land uses are illegal.

Legal experts disagree as to how much protection the *Lucas* decision gives landowners who face regulations that affect the value of their property. Nevertheless, *Lucas* is significant because, as author Jay Feinman pointed out, it "did signal the Court's willingness to expand the takings doctrine into the realm of what traditionally had been valid police power regulation."[*]

[*]Jay M. Feinman, *Law 101: Everything You Need to Know About the American Legal System.* New York: Oxford University Press, 2000, p. 245.

The loss on the resale of the lots, plus the legal and other fees associated with the lawsuit itself, cost South Carolina's taxpayers about $3 million.

It has also been argued that the regulatory process favors special interests at the expense of the public as a whole. Karol Ceplo, a professor at Clemson University, believes that a small group of activists persuaded Congress to pass sweeping environmental laws that burden thousands of property owners. Ceplo explained,

> The environmental lobby, populated by individuals with higher than average incomes and stronger preferences for wetlands protection, discovered its political strength in the late 1970s and used that strength to impose the costs of environmental protection on politically weak property owners, who are widely dispersed across the country.[51]

Regulations single out the "unlucky few."

The Supreme Court has stated that the purpose of the Takings Clause is "to bar Government from forcing some people alone to bear public burdens which, in all fairness and justice, should be borne by the public as a whole."[52] One of the strongest objections to land-use regulations is that a few unlucky landowners suffer a heavy and disproportionate economic burden in order to benefit the public as a whole. In New York City, the owners of about 400 parcels of land were prevented from developing them because city officials had declared the buildings on them historic landmarks that could not be altered or removed without permission.

Lee Ann Welch, a contributor to a book about the property-rights movement, told the story of another unlucky landowner, Benjamin Cone Jr., who owned 7,200 acres of timberland in North Carolina. Welch described him as a good steward of the land who actively supported efforts to clean up the environment and protect plant and animal life. Federal regulators, however, declared one-fifth of his land off-limits to logging because it was found to be a habitat for an endangered bird. According to an appraiser, the land was worth only about 4 percent of what it would have been had the birds not lived there. The total loss of value was more than $2 million, or almost $74,000 for each of the 29 birds on Cone's land. Cone was also forced to incur other costs, such as hiring experts to ensure that his use of the land complied with the Endangered Species Act.

Critics of environmental laws maintain that they are counterproductive because they are inflexible and enforced on a "top-down" basis and are often based on political ideology rather than on facts. For example, a provision of the Clean Water Act requires owners of property that contains protected wetlands to get a permit before filling them. Federal officials have interpreted the act so broadly that, as Justice Antonin Scalia observed, they have applied it to "storm drains, roadside ditches, ripples of sand in the desert that may contain water once a year, and lands that are covered by floodwaters once every 100 years."[53] Making matters worse is that many environmental laws are so open-ended that property owners are unsure as to when their use of their land will result in heavy penalties—penalties imposed after the fact. Property-rights advocates also question the motives of environmentalists. Some, in their view, are biased against progress and even place the interests of plants and animals above those of human beings.

The costs of land-use regulations outweigh their benefits.

Property-rights advocates contend that environmental regulations rely too heavily on the "stick" of penalties and not enough on the "carrot" of incentives. In the case of the Endangered Species Act, Lee Ann Welch argued that "the government is not protecting species but is instead contributing to their destruction by angering and alienating the private landowner with the perverse incentives contained in the Endangered Species Act."[54]

Jesse Walker, a fellow at the Competitive Enterprise Institute, went even farther. He argued that the act encourages unscrupulous land owners to destroy endangered creatures:

"Exactions" Come Under Scrutiny: *Nollan* and *Dolan*

Two U.S. Supreme Court decisions in cases that involved exactions—that is, government-imposed conditions that an owner must meet in order to improve his or her property—signaled the Court's increasing willingness to view land-use regulations as "takings." The first case, *Nollan v. California Coastal Commission*, 483 U.S. 825 (1987), arose when James and Marilyn Nollan asked the California Coastal Commission for a permit to build a larger home on their beachfront lot. The commission refused to issue a permit unless the Nollans allowed the public to pass across a strip of their property. It was concerned that a larger structure would block the view of the beach and add to the impression that the beach was not open to the public.

By a 5 to 4 majority, the Court held that the public-access condition was an unconstitutional taking of the Nollans' property. Justice Antonin Scalia, who wrote the majority opinion, concluded that there had to be an "essential nexus" between a condition attached to a building permit and the state interest that the condition would serve. In this case, Justice Scalia found that the commission's concerns about public access to the beach were "utterly unrelated" to the public-access requirement it imposed on the Nollans. He wrote:

> It is quite impossible to understand how a requirement that people already on the public beaches be able to walk across the Nollans' property reduces any obstacles to viewing the beach created by the new house. It is also impossible to understand how it lowers any "psychological barrier" to using the public beaches, or how it helps to remedy any additional congestion on them caused by construction of the Nollans' new house.

In his dissenting opinion, Justice William Brennan criticized the majority for having resurrected "strict scrutiny" of police-power regulation—a standard that had been discredited long ago. Justice Brennan maintained that, even assuming that an essential nexus was required by the Constitution, one was present because of the impact that the Nollans' larger home would have on access to the beach. He also argued that the public-access condition was not a taking because it was a minimal burden and because the commission had imposed the same condition on other property owners in the area.

Say you own some land and plan to build a house on it. One day you come across a northern spotted owl, a Delhi Sands flower-loving fly, or the rare and precious San Francisco

The second case, *Dolan v. City of Tigard*, 512 U.S. 374 (1994), began when Florence Dolan asked her city's planning commission for a permit to expand her store and redevelop her property. Although the improvements complied with the zoning ordinance, the commission refused to issue a permit unless she "dedicated"—gave the public access to—a strip of her land for use as a floodplain and a pedestrian and bicycle path.

Dolan sued the city. Her case reached the Supreme Court which, by a 5 to 4 vote, held that the dedication requirement was an unconstitutional taking. In his majority opinion, Chief Justice William Rehnquist announced a two-part test for determining whether exactions were constitutional. First, as the Court ruled in *Nollan*, there had to be an essential nexus between the exaction and a legitimate state interest. Second, there also had to be "rough proportionality"; in other words, the government "must make some sort of individualized determination that the required dedication is related both in nature and extent to the impact of the proposed development."

Although the city had legitimate interests in easing traffic congestion and preventing flooding, the chief justice concluded that it had not proven that the restrictions it placed on Dolan's permit were proportional to those interests. He found that proof of proportionality was necessary because the property right in question—the right to exclude others from Dolan's land—was substantial. The chief justice described that right as "one of the most essential sticks in the bundle of rights that are commonly characterized as property."

Justice John Paul Stevens dissented. He disagreed with the proportionality requirement because it required city officials to prove that exactions were constitutional. That approach, he argued, was contrary to the Court's traditional approach of presuming that the government had acted in a constitutional manner. Justice Stevens also criticized the majority for having focused exclusively on Dolan's property rights rather than examining the transaction as a whole, which would result in a net gain to her. Because of the benefits to Dolan and the fact that the city had not physically seized her property, he concluded that no taking had occurred. Finally, Justice Stevens argued that the exaction in this case should be viewed as a form of business regulation. He suggested that commercial developers of property were on a different legal footing than a citizen "defending hearth and home against the king's intrusion."

Mome Rat. Under the ESA, it's in your interest to dispose of the beast before the government gets wind of it and blocks your plans. Even if you don't have any plans, you still might want to kill the creature lest it someday wipe out the value of your property.[55]

The act has also imposed costs on all Americans. For example, measures aimed at saving the habitat of the northern spotted owl had a financial and social impact on Native Americans who lived in the area, cost local governments a substantial amount of tax revenue, and drove up the price of lumber—which homeowners and businesses everywhere eventually have to pay. The act's benefits appear minimal. Critics point out that only 20 of the 1,354 species placed on the endangered list were later removed from it. Eight species were listed by mistake, seven became extinct, and three of the five successes occurred on a single island in the Pacific Ocean.

Summary

A wide range of laws that do not involve the physical seizure of property nevertheless reduce its value, sometimes by a substantial amount. Property-rights advocates contend that those laws are "takings" and that affected property owners should be compensated. Many laws, especially those aimed at protecting the environment, require a small minority of property owners to bear the economic burden, and the benefits of some laws are either difficult to measure or do not exist. Administrators who enforce the laws sometimes make bad decisions because they are not responsible for the economic consequences of their actions.

Land-use Restrictions Are in the Public Interest

L and-use regulation is an exercise of the police power, which is, in effect, the government's power to protect its citizens. In his opinion in *Mugler v. Kansas*, 1887, Justice John Harlan explained why government needed the police power:

> Power to determine such questions, so as to bind all, must exist somewhere; else society will be at the mercy of the few, who, regarding only their own appetites or passions, may be willing to imperil the peace and security of the many, provided only they are permitted to do as they please.[56]

Since then, the Supreme Court has held that the police power authorizes the government not only to regulate uses of property that are "noxious" but also to impose restrictions that are "reasonably related to the implementation of a policy—not unlike historic preservation—expected to produce a widespread public benefit and applicable to all similarly situated property."[57]

Property rights are not absolute.

In 1893, historian Frederick Jackson Turner wrote a classic book entitled *The Significance of the Frontier in American History*. In that book, he celebrated the character traits that made it possible to build a nation out of wilderness. Those traits included what Turner called "dominant individualism." The pioneer spirit lives on to this day in the form of owners who believe they can do whatever they wish with their own land.

Despite that commonly held belief, people have never been free to use their property as they pleased. In his concurring opinion in *Lucas*, Justice Anthony Kennedy observed that

> property is bought and sold, investments are made, subject to the State's power to regulate. Where a taking is alleged from regulations which deprive the property of all value, the test must be whether the deprivation is contrary to reasonable, investment-backed expectations.[58]

Justice Kennedy was not announcing a new principle of law. Nearly two centuries earlier, New York's highest court stated that

> every right, from an absolute ownership in property, down to a mere easement, is purchased and holden [sic] subject to the restriction that it shall be so exercised as not to injure others. Though, at the time, it be remote and inoffensive, the purchaser is bound to know, at his peril, that it may become otherwise.[59]

In his dissenting opinion in *Nollan v. California Coastal Commission*, Justice William Brennan quoted from a law review article that made the point that one person's use of land affected other owners' welfare:

Property does not exist in isolation. Particular parcels are tied to one another in complex ways, and property is more accurately described as being inextricably part of a network of relationships that is neither limited to, nor usefully defined by, the property boundaries with which the legal system is accustomed to dealing. Frequently, use of any given parcel of property is at the same time effectively a use of, or a demand upon, property beyond the border of the user.[60]

The more intensely a landowner develops his property, the more likely it is to have an impact on the community, such as added pollution or traffic or an overall decline in the quality of life that attracted residents in the first place. For that reason, local officials often place a condition on development: In exchange for a building permit, the owner must give something back to the community, such as allowing the public to use part of his land. These conditions are known in the law as "exactions." Although the United States Supreme Court has begun to scrutinize exactions more closely, it nevertheless approves of them in principle.

Landowners who support regulatory taking laws in effect want the rest of society to pay them to comply with the law. As Justice Harlan wrote in *Mugler*, however, "No legislature can bargain away the public health or the public morals. The people themselves cannot do it, much less their servants."[61]

Market forces alone cannot protect the public.

The philosophy advanced by property-rights advocates draws heavily from Adam Smith's classic 1776 work, *The Wealth of Nations*. Smith popularized the "invisible hand," the idea that, when individuals act in their own self-interest, society ultimately benefits. A professor at the University of California at Santa Barbara, Garret Hardin, argued that the opposite is true. He maintained that self-interested actions actually harm society. Harden used the example of a "commons," a pasture that is open to all herdsmen. A self-interested herdsman who increased the size of his herd would enjoy almost all the benefits of adding animals but would suffer only a small fraction of the harm that a larger herd inflicted on society. Those self-interested decisions eventually would lead to disaster. Hardin explained,

> Therein is the tragedy. Each man is locked into a system that compels him to increase his herd without limit—in a world

Police Power Upheld: *Mugler v. Kansas*

Long before the Eighteenth Amendment imposed Prohibition nationally, a number of states elected to "go dry." One of them was Kansas. In 1880, voters approved a law that prohibited the manufacture and sale of alcoholic beverages. Some Kansas brewers closed their doors. Others defied the law and ran the risk of criminal prosecution or of having their businesses closed down as public nuisances.

The owners of two breweries filed suits that challenged Kansas's Prohibition law. They did not attack the law head-on but instead maintained that it deprived them of their property in violation of the Due Process Clause of the Fourteenth Amendment to the Constitution. The brewery owners argued that they constructed their breweries when alcohol was legal and, because their breweries could not be put to a different use, they had lost most of their investment. Thus the brewery owners made what today is called a "regulatory taking" argument.

The case went to the United States Supreme Court, which, in *Mugler v. Kansas*, 123 U.S. 623 (1887), unanimously rejected the brewers' argument. Justice John Harlan wrote the court's opinion. He first pointed out that, decades earlier, the Court had concluded that state liquor-control laws were valid exercises of the police power aimed at protecting the public from the harmful effects of drinking. He observed, "It belongs to [state legislatures] to exert what are known as the police powers of the state, and to determine, primarily, what measures are appropriate or needful for the protection of the public morals, the public health, or the public safety."

Justice Harlan concluded that the Due Process Clause did not require the government to compensate property owners for the consequences of police-power regulations. He observed that "all property in this country is held under the implied obligation that the owner's use of it shall not be injurious to the community." Although the making and selling of beer were legal at the time that

that is limited. Ruin is the destination toward which all men rush, each pursuing his own best interest in a society that believes in the freedom of the commons. Freedom in a commons brings ruin to all.[62]

Hardin went on to argue that there were some instances in which the government had to use its regulatory power:

the brewers went into business, Kansas had not offered them any assurance that those activities would remain legal. Given the extent to which the liquor industry was regulated, Justice Harlan concluded that the brewers had a weak claim to what modern courts call an "investment-backed expectation" that might support a claim of a regulatory taking.

Justice Harlan did recognize that there were "limits beyond which legislation cannot rightfully go," and he stated that a law that had "no real or substantial relation" to the public health, safety, or morals or that was "a palpable invasion of rights secured by the fundamental law" could not stand. He did not elaborate, however, forcing the legal community to guess the limits of the police power. Critics argue that Justice Harlan's opinion laid the foundation for later Court decisions that recognized virtually no limits on that power.

Justice Stephen Field dissented in part. Although Kansas had the power to regulate liquor within its borders, he maintained that it could not bar the brewing of beer to be sold in states in which it was legal. He also contended that Kansas's power to enforce Prohibition did not extend beyond closing the brewery. In his view, state authorities should not have destroyed the beer itself, which could be legally sold for some purposes (for example, as medicine), or the bottles, glasses, and other items that could be put to other, lawful uses.

Justice Field's concurrence anticipated an issue that arose during the twentieth century, especially after the government intensified its fight against illegal drugs. One legal tool that authorities nowadays rely on is *civil forfeiture*, a procedure under which the government asks a court for permission to confiscate "instrumentalities of crime," such as a vehicle used to transport illegal drugs. Because the procedure is civil in nature—the property itself is the "defendant"—the government may confiscate property even if its owner is never found guilty of, or even charged with, a crime.

> But the air and waters surrounding us cannot readily be
> fenced, and so the tragedy of the commons as a cesspool must
> be prevented by different means, by coercive laws or taxing
> devices that make it cheaper for the polluter to treat his pol-
> lutants than to discharge them untreated.[63]

Since Hardin's article appeared, his "commons" analogy has
also been applied to coastal property and habitat for plants
and animals in support of the argument that regulations are
necessary.

Sometimes, free-market forces lead to outcomes that benefit
a select few while the rest of society suffers. That is often true
with the environment. It is difficult to put a dollar value on,
for example, the loss of species, the disappearance of natural
beauty, and the effects of air and water pollution on health. As
David Malin Roodman, a senior researcher at the WorldWatch
Institute, observed:

> Laws, not market forces alone, are what will protect endan-
> gered species, manage nuclear waste, and ban pollutants that
> may be deemed unacceptable in any amount, such as DDT or
> dioxins. Waste incinerators, as long as they are built, are likely
> to be disproportionately located in poor and minority neigh-
> borhoods unless these communities have the legal means to
> protect themselves.[64]

Critics exaggerate the impact of land-use regulation.

Just as opponents of eminent domain point to Susette Kelo's
eviction from her home as a symbol of condemnation abuse,
property-rights advocates cite "horror stories" to support their
argument that land-use regulations such the Endangered Species
Act are unfair. According to the Environmental Defense Fund,
however, critics have painted a misleading picture of how the act
is enforced: "Of the thousands of projects or actions reviewed by

the federal government each year, fewer than 1 in 1000 cannot be altered or modified to reduce their impacts on endangered species to acceptable levels."[65]

Furthermore, the government is willing to work with landowners to find a solution that would permit the project in question but protect endangered species. The landowner might agree, for example, to dedicate other land as habitat or to make a contribution to researchers who are working to preserve the species. The same is true of wetlands restrictions. In his dissenting opinion in *Rapanos v. United States*, Justice John Paul Stevens disagreed with the assumption that the cost of preserving wetlands was too high. He pointed out that "these costs amount to only a small fraction of 1% of the $760 billion spent each year on private and public construction and development activity."[66] In addition, he observed that "the fact that large investments are required to finance large developments merely means that those who are most adversely affected . . . are persons who have the ability to communicate effectively with their representatives."[67]

"Regulatory takings" measures are dangerous.

In 2004, Oregon voters approved Measure 37, a law aimed at compensating property owners for the loss of value caused by regulation. Ray Ring, a writer for *High Country News*, explained how far-reaching that measure is:

> Here's how the initiatives would work: If you could fit 20 houses on your land, plus a junkyard, a gravel mine, and a lemonade stand, and the government limits you to six houses and lemonade, then the government would have to pay you whatever profit you would have made on the unbuilt 14 houses, junkyard and mine. Generally, if the government can't or won't pay you, then it would have to drop the regulations.[68]

Measure 37 has already caused serious disruption to Oregon's system of land-use regulation. As of July 2006, property owners

Land-use Regulation Ruled Not a Taking:
Penn Central Transportation Company v. New York City

In an effort to preserve historic structures, New York City passed an ordinance that required owners of designated "landmarks" to get approval from the city's Landmarks Commission before making alterations to them. In an effort to offset the financial impact of the restrictions, the ordinance also provided financial incentives to the landmarks' owners.

Grand Central Terminal, the famous railroad station in Manhattan, was one of about 400 structures designated landmarks. Penn Central Transportation Company, which owned the terminal, asked the Landmarks Commission for permission to build a 55-story office tower above it. The commission denied the request because it found that the tower was so massive that it would overwhelm the terminal. Penn Central then filed suit against the city. It argued that the ordinance amounted to a taking of the air rights above the terminal. The lawsuit reached the United States Supreme Court which, in *Penn Central Transportation Company v. New York City*, 438 U.S. 104 (1978), concluded that no taking had occurred. The vote was 6 to 3.

Justice William Brennan wrote the majority opinion. Justice Brennan first observed that the Court had never laid down a hard-and-fast rule as to when a regulation amounted to a taking. He set out three more or less open-ended standards: (1) the character of the regulation, (2) its economic impact on the property owner, and (3) the extent to which it interfered with "the distinct, investment-backed expectations" of the owner.

In this case, Justice Brennan concluded that the ordinance was a legitimate exercise of the city's police power. Penn Central had conceded that the city's objective of preserving historic structures was valid and that restricting the alteration or improvement of those structures was an appropriate means of achieving that objective. Because the ordinance was expected to produce a public benefit, he found it similar to land-use regulations that the Court had earlier upheld as constitutional.

Justice Brennan disagreed with Penn Central's contention that the city's action amounted to a taking of its air rights over the terminal. He rejected the idea that rights in a parcel of land could be divided in such a way as to transform a loss of value into a taking, writing that " 'taking' jurisprudence does not divide a single parcel into discrete segments and attempt to determine whether rights in a particular segment have been entirely abrogated." Justice Brennan also concluded that the ordinance did not result in the taking of the terminal as a whole, because Penn Central could still make use of the terminal itself and qualified for financial incentives as well. In addition, Justice Brennan noted that Penn Central might have won approval for a more modest structure but instead went to court to challenge the ordinance.

Although the historic-landmark ordinance was a novel form of zoning, Justice Brennan upheld it as constitutional. In response to Penn Central's claim that it amounted to "reverse spot zoning"—zoning that arbitrarily singled out parcels of land for less-favorable treatment than neighboring ones—he wrote, "It is, of course, true that the Landmarks Law has a more severe impact on some landowners than on others, but that, in itself, does not mean that the law effects a 'taking.' Legislation designed to promote the general welfare commonly burdens some more than others." Justice Brennan also concluded that "aesthetic" zoning—that is, zoning aimed at preserving the appearance of a neighborhood—was not by its nature arbitrary. He noted that the Court had approved such zoning in the past and added that Landmarks Commission rulings could be appealed to the courts, which were capable of reviewing them for arbitrariness.

Justice William Rehnquist dissented. He maintained that the ordinance could be called "zoning" only in the broadest sense of that word because only a small fraction of the city's one million structures had been designated landmarks. He went on to argue that the ordinance resulted in no "average reciprocity of advantage," in which restrictions on land use not only benefit the community as a whole but also the owners whose use of land was restricted. In this case, a relatively few individual buildings, all separated from one another, were singled out and treated differently; therefore, no such reciprocity existed. Justice Rehnquist also observed that a regulation that singled out a small group of landowners to bear a substantial financial burden was "precisely [the] sort of discrimination that the Fifth Amendment prohibits."

In Justice Rehnquist's view, the landmark ordinance was a taking. Unlike exercises of the police power that the Court had upheld in the past, the ordinance was not limited to "noxious" uses of property. Instead, it was a taking of the air rights over Grand Central Terminal. Because Penn Central was entitled to compensation for the lost air rights, Justice Rehnquist insisted that the case should have been sent back to the New York courts to determine whether the incentives offered under the ordinance were "a full and perfect equivalent."

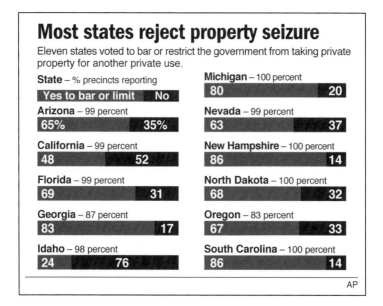

Most states reject property seizure

Eleven states voted to bar or restrict the government from taking private property for another private use.

State – % precincts reporting		
Yes to bar or limit		**No**

Arizona – 99 percent
65% 35%

California – 99 percent
48 52

Florida – 99 percent
69 31

Georgia – 87 percent
83 17

Idaho – 98 percent
24 76

Michigan – 100 percent
80 20

Nevada – 99 percent
63 37

New Hampshire – 100 percent
86 14

North Dakota – 100 percent
68 32

Oregon – 83 percent
67 33

South Carolina – 100 percent
86 14

AP

In the wake of the *Kelo* decision, several states put the issue of eminent domain up for a ballot initiative, allowing citizens to vote on whether they would allow their states to use the power of eminent domain. The November 2006 elections showed that in 11 states voters chose to ban or restrict the government from taking private land for another private use.

had filed 2,700 claims asking for $4 billion in compensation, and state and local officials have waived enforcement of land-use regulations in order to settle hundreds of lawsuits brought under the new law.

That every owner has the right to the "highest and best use" of his or her property—that is, the most profitable use possible—is a dramatic change in the American approach to land use. John Schmidt, who served as associate attorney general in the Clinton administration, said of property-rights measures, "[They] are based on a radical premise that has never been a part of our law or tradition: that a private property owner has the absolute right to the greatest possible profit from that property, regardless of the consequences of the proposed use on other individuals or the public generally."[69] No justices of the Supreme Court, even the aggressively probusiness justices who sat on it during the 1920s, have endorsed such a radical proposition.

Furthermore, critics allege that regulatory-takings measures would primarily benefit wealthy developers and provide little relief to individual homeowners. For that reason, they contend, sponsors of those measures have resorted to deception. Oliver Griswold, a spokesman for the Ballot Initiative Strategy Center, commented on the property-rights measures that went before voters in 2006: "[Conservatives are] using the reaction to *Kelo* to slip in these takings measures. . . . It totally decimates a municipality's ability to plan for growth in the future. And it has nothing to do with a government taking grandma's house."[70]

The property-rights movement is an attack on government itself.

In *Pennsylvania Coal Company v. Mahon*, 1922, Justice Oliver Wendell Holmes warned, "Government hardly could go on if to some extent values incident to property could not be diminished without paying for every such change in the general law. As long recognized, some values are enjoyed under an implied limitation and must yield to the police power."[71] Some argue that the police power—if not government itself—is under attack from property-rights activists. They believe that the real objective is, as conservative activist Grover Norquist once said, "to get [government] down to the size where we can drown it in the bathtub."[72]

Glenn Sugameli, a lawyer with the National Wildlife Federation, argued that property-rights measures could provide the basis for undermining laws, such as the Civil Rights Act of 1964 and the Americans With Disabilities Act, that are so widely accepted that an effort to repeal them would almost certainly

"The Tragedy of the Commons": Can We Live Without Regulation?

In 1968, Garrett Hardin, a biology professor at the University of California at Santa Barbara, wrote an article in which he argued that the time had come for the government to use its regulatory power to curb overpopulation. Hardin analogized the planet to a medieval "commons," a pasture that was open to all herdsmen. He argued that, when herdsmen acted in their individual best interests—which human beings are prone to do—the entire community eventually suffered. Hardin explained, "As a rational being, each herdsman seeks to maximize his gain. Explicitly or implicitly, more or less consciously, he asks, 'What is the utility *to me* of adding one more animal to my herd?'"

That utility has a positive component and a negative one. Because the herdsman reaps almost all the benefits of adding to his herd but shares the negative effects of overgrazing with all of the other herdsmen, the positive greatly outweighs the negative. It therefore makes sense for him to keep as many animals as possible. His doing so, however, leads to "tragedy," which Hardin defines as the "the remorseless working of things." He explained, "Each man is locked into a system that compels him to increase his herd without limit—in a world that is limited. Ruin is the destination toward which all men rush, each pursuing his own best interest in a society that believes in the freedom of the commons. Freedom in a commons brings ruin to all."

To avert the tragedy, Hardin argued for "enclosure"—that is, regulations on use of the commons. He called for regulation because most people's consciences are not strong enough to discourage selfish behavior. Hardin also argued that, as population grows and competition for resources becomes more intense, new forms of regulation become necessary. He also made the counterintuitive argument that freedom and regulation go hand in hand: "When men mutually agreed to pass laws against robbing, mankind became more free, not less so. Individuals locked into the logic of the commons are free only to bring on universal ruin; once they see the necessity of mutual coercion, they become free to pursue other goals."

Hardin's "commons" analogy has been extended to social problems that range from pollution (which he also mentioned in his essay) to spam e-mails and urban graffiti. His analogy also can be applied to land-use issues such as controlling sprawl and protecting the habitat of endangered species.

Although "The Tragedy of the Commons" is generally considered a case for regulation, some insist that it is really an argument for better-defined property rights and for market-based approaches to the management of scarce resources. One idea advanced by free-market advocates is the "Coasian" solution, under which individuals who make excessive use of the commons are obligated to pay those who do not. The Coasian solution places a dollar value on the negative effects of overuse and forces individuals to consider those effects before acting. The result, at least in theory, is that people would behave differently than the herdsmen in an unregulated commons.

fail. Sugameli quoted former Solicitor General Charles Fried, who revealed property-rights activists' true agenda:

> The grand plan was to make government pay compensation as for a taking of property every time its regulations impinged too severely on a property right—limiting the possible uses for a parcel of land or restricting or tying up a business in regulatory red tape. If the government labored under so severe an obligation, there would be, to say the least, much less regulation.[73]

Sugameli warned that regulatory-takings measures "could reverse the results of cases in which courts have rejected takings claims brought by businesses affected by local efforts to protect people, property, and communities by controlling drunk driving, drinking in public, and all-night bars."[74]

Summary

Property rights are not absolute and never have been regarded as absolute. American courts hold that a person owns property on the condition that he or she will not harm others. Government places restrictions on land use in order to prevent harmful uses in the first place. It is sometimes necessary for the government to regulate because unrestricted property use can deplete natural resources, harm the environment, or interfere with others' use and enjoyment of their own property. Critics of land-use regulations exaggerate their negative impact in order to gain public support for measures that would weaken them. Those measures will, in the long run, cause more harm than good to the public.

Zoning Harms Property Owners and Provides Few Benefits to Society

C ritics argue that zoning restrictions in most American communities go well beyond their original intent of regulating "noxious" uses of property. Nancie Marzulla observed that they have expanded to include "historic preservation, battlefield protection, scenic designations, setbacks along waterways and streams, farmland protection, establishment of 'greenways,' buffer zones, designation of parks and preserves, and restrictions on natural-resource development."[75]

There is merit to banning development near scenic locations such as a beachfront or to making a community more attractive by requiring owners of historic structures to preserve them. Many believe that government should achieve these goals through eminent domain and financial incentives, however, not through regulations that force property owners to bear all the cost. That is especially true when the benefits of regulation are difficult to measure or will materialize far in the future.

The government misuses zoning.

Zoning was originally viewed as an extension of nuisance law. Erin O'Hara, a law professor at George Mason University, contended that "the nuisance rationale, originally intended to justify uncompensated restriction of only the most noxious or illegal uses, has, by virtue of [language] from even the earliest cases, been extended to include any harmful use of property, as determined by the state itself."[76] Some maintain that this trend is the result of courts having given public officials overly broad power to define property as "blighted" and to declare certain land uses "harmful."

Property-rights advocates maintain that many zoning restrictions apply to uses of property that do not invade others' rights. Roger Pilon of the Cato Institute explained, "If some 'public good' is indeed achieved by those restrictions—if a scenic view, for example, is a public good—then let the public pay for that good rather than take it from some individual member of the public."[77] Pilon also argued that zoning restrictions that regulate the appearance of property rather than prevent harmful uses of it are illegitimate.

Some zoning restrictions are so arbitrary that those who cannot use their land as they wish gain few, if any, benefits in return. The principle of "reciprocity of advantage," historically an important benefit of zoning, has disappeared. In his dissenting opinion in *Penn Central Transportation Company v. New York City*, Justice William Rehnquist explained:

> Where a relatively few individual buildings, all separated from one another, are singled out and treated differently from surrounding buildings, no such reciprocity exists. The cost to the property owner which results from the imposition of restrictions applicable only to his property and not that of his

neighbors may be substantial—in this case, several million dollars—with no comparable reciprocal benefits.[78]

Some communities have misused zoning ordinances and other land-use restrictions to drive out property owners that they consider undesirable. Steven Greenhut cited the example of Elsinore, California, where officials used building code violations as a pretext for condemning property so that it could be used for a high-end development. Greenhut also asserted that local officials have arbitrarily enforced their zoning ordinances in an effort to pressure landowners, such as churches, to sell to someone who would pay more in property taxes.

Zoning laws are not consistently enforced.

One criticism of zoning is that local officials make too many exceptions to restrictions that are meant to be uniform. The typical zoning ordinance requires a person who seeks a *variance*—an exemption from some requirements of the ordinance—to show the zoning board of appeals that strict compliance would create practical difficulties that go beyond mere inconvenience. Planning expert Herbert Smith, however, has contended that 95 percent of variances fail to meet the legal standard. He went on to explain why:

> Many communities adopt the position that a variance is the preferred way to operate, under the misguided belief that it is easier to deal with individual problems than it is to say no and preserve the integrity of a zoning ordinance; after all, not everybody is going to want to ask to do something similar anyway.[79]

These wrongly-granted variances are seldom challenged in court because communities rarely sue their own officials and few residents consider a legal challenge worth their time and money. As a result, Smith explained:

> Most boards of adjustment grant special privileges to applicants. They allow something to occur on one lot that all other

"Exclusionary Zoning": *Southern Burlington County N.A.A.C.P. v. Township of Mount Laurel*

The township of Mt. Laurel, New Jersey, was one of many communities that grew rapidly after World War II as people fled cities for fast-growing suburbs. In an effort to control the pace of that growth, township officials adopted a strict zoning ordinance.

Some, however, argued that Mt. Laurel had "zoned out" people who were not wealthy. A group of plaintiffs, most of whom were African American or Latino, challenged the township's zoning ordinance on the ground that it excluded low- and moderate-income families. Mt. Laurel replied that New Jersey's tax structure, which forced communities to rely on property taxes to fund their public schools, gave them no choice but to attract residents who had the money to buy expensive homes and, at the same time, had few or no school-age children. The case reached the Supreme Court of New Jersey, which, in *Southern Burlington County N.A.A.C.P. v. Township of Mount Laurel*, 67 N.J. 151, 336 A.2d 713 (N.J. Sup. Ct. 1975), ruled unanimously that the zoning ordinance was unconstitutional. Justice Fred Hall wrote the opinion of the court.

Justice Hall noted that exclusionary zoning was not unique to Mt. Laurel and that it also affected a broad class of individuals: "We have reference to young and elderly couples, single persons, and large, growing families not in the poverty class, but who still cannot afford the only kinds of housing realistically permitted in most places—relatively high-priced, single-family detached dwellings on sizeable lots and, in some municipalities, expensive apartments." He added that suburbanization and restrictive zoning trapped the poor in cities where jobs continued to disappear and the quality of housing grew worse.

Turning to Mt. Laurel's ordinance, Justice Hall found that it essentially barred residences other than single-family detached homes. Although township officials had acted for financial reasons, not out of an intent to discriminate on the basis of race, origin, or "believed social incompatibility," he found that the ordinance nonetheless had a discriminatory effect. Because Mt. Laurel's zoning ordinance made it "physically and economically impossible" to provide low- and moderate-income housing, Justice Hall presumed that it violated the substantive due process and equal protection clauses of the New Jersey Constitution. "Presumed" means that a community could offer a justification for its zoning restrictions. Justice Hall found that the state's tax structure was no excuse for exclusionary zoning, however.

(continues on next page)

landowners in like circumstances are not permitted to do by right, without a true showing that denial would deprive the owner of a legitimate use of property. If I want to add a room to my house, thus infringing on the open space requirements for the lot, and am given the variance I request to do so, everyone else in that zoning district should expect to be able to do the same thing.[80]

The end result, Smith warned, is "variance abuse," which invites legal challenges by those who are denied variances and undermines the entire zoning ordinance.

(continues from previous page)

Having found Mt. Laurel's zoning ordinance unconstitutional, Justice Hall ordered township officials to "make realistically possible the opportunity for an appropriate variety and choice of housing for all categories of people who may desire to live there." Measures that would accomplish that goal included permitting multifamily housing and eliminating "artificial and unjustifiable" minimum home- and lot-size requirements. Justice Hall went on to conclude that exclusionary zoning must be addressed on a regionwide basis and that every growing community in the region had to assume its fair share of accommodating low- and middle-income families. He observed that communities had acted in their own "selfish" and "parochial" interest in zoning matters and in effect built walls around themselves to keep out those who could not add to the tax base. As a result, a community's exclusionary zoning had an effect on the welfare of citizens who lived outside its boundaries.

In his concurring opinion, Justice Morris Pashman argued that the court should have gone even farther and imposed a broad rule that would govern zoning decisions statewide. He also called for "forceful judicial intervention" in light of the already widespread use of exclusionary zoning; the motivations behind it, including unwillingness to pay the costs of suburban development and a desire to stay homogeneous; a national shortage of affordable housing; and the lasting effects of exclusionary zoning on the character of a community. He also cited the value of cultural pluralism in suburban communities:

It has also been argued that the zoning process favors the rich and powerful. New forms of zoning, which involve large tracts of land on which multiple structures will be built, require the participation of large developers that have a decided advantage over the average citizen in the planning and zoning process. These businesses can afford to hire the best legal and land-use experts and have appeared before local officials many times in the past. Herbert Smith explained how developers can hijack the zoning process:

> They march in a troop of professionals and experts with charts, slides, and fancy, colored drawings. A parade of wit-

A homogeneous community, one exhibiting almost total similarities of taste, habit, custom and behavior is culturally dead, aside from being downright boring. New and different life styles, habits and customs are the lifeblood of America. They are its strength, its growth force. Just as diversity strengthens and enriches the country as a whole, so will it strengthen and enrich a suburban community.

Although the court gave Mt. Laurel 90 days to eliminate the discriminatory provisions of its zoning ordinance, legal proceedings dragged on for years. After the court's decision, exclusionary-zoning suits were filed against numerous other communities in the state. Appeals in several of these cases eventually forced the justices to revisit the issue of exclusionary zoning in *Southern Burlington County N.A.A.C.P. v. Township of Mount Laurel*, 92 N.J. 158, 456 A.2d 390 (N.J. Sup. Ct. 1983), commonly called *Mount Laurel II*. The justices found that many communities had been slow to comply with the first *Mount Laurel* decision. As a result, they decided to use stronger measures against noncomplying communities. The most controversial feature of *Mount Laurel II* was the "builder's remedy," under which a homebuilder could file suit to override exclusionary zoning requirements.

Two years after *Mount Laurel II*, the New Jersey legislature passed the Fair Housing Act, which attempted to legislate a statewide solution to the problem of affordable housing. To accomplish that goal, the act created an administrative agency that had the authority to spell out each community's obligation to provide its fair share of affordable housing.

nesses testify how important the proposal is to the future of the community, the taxes it will produce, and that the variance will have no adverse effect upon the area or the intent and purpose of any adopted plan or the zoning ordinance. In most instances, they have done their homework well and propagandized the neighborhood in order to convince any objectors not to appear.[81]

Some property-rights advocates even compare developers to the "robber barons" of the nineteenth century.

Zoning is based on obsolete notions of planning.

Critics argue that zoning, which became popular during the Progressive Era of the early twentieth century, has outlived its usefulness. The Progressives believed that central planning, carried out by a trained corps of specialists, could cure a variety of social problems. The failure of many urban-renewal and economic-redevelopment projects has shown that central planning rarely succeeds, however. Steven Greenhut explained that central planning is a poor substitute for a free market:

> The marketplace is not some force of nature, as critics depict it. It is the sum total of the private decisions every individual makes. It is not cold and heartless, as some depict it. The market is us—and it's a far more reliable way to drive decisions, including those about the use of property and the type of business that should occupy a site, than letting central planners make them.[82]

Critics also accuse land-use planners of being elitist. One such critic, author Jane Jacobs, observed that "as in all Utopias, the right to have plans of any significance belonged only to the planners in charge."[83] Planners have also been accused of disrespect toward their fellow citizens. Professor Robert Bruegmann stated that "many members of cultural elites are not interested in hearing about the benefits of increased choice for the population at large because they believe that ordinary citizens, given a choice, will usually make the wrong one."[84] Bruegmann also pointed out that, although Americans live in cleaner, greener, and safer communities than those of their great-grandparents, planners call those communities "sprawl" and look for ways to outlaw it. He added, "At very least, it seems to me, our highly dispersed urban regions deserve some respectful attention before we jump to the conclusion that they are terrible places that need to be totally transformed."[85]

On balance, zoning provides few benefits.

Professor Bruegmann suggested that the effects of zoning might be overstated because ordinances largely reflect market-driven decisions about where to live and what land to develop. He pointed to Houston, which is unusual in that it never had a zoning ordinance. Residents of that city have relied instead on voluntary measures, such as deed restrictions that regulated how property could be used and even who could live there. Bruegmann observed that "most parts of Houston . . . look and function very much like corresponding parts of other cities developed at the same time."[86] That was so because a homeowner could go to court at the first sign of unlawful land use. Bruegmann added that zoning has created, rather than controlled, sprawl: "Large-lot zoning, particularly favored since the 1960s, almost certainly forced many homeowners to buy more land than they otherwise would have wanted, leading to lower densities than would have been the case without the regulations."[87]

He added that new zoning tools have resulted in "developments [that,] like the suburbs of many European cities, could be seen as sprawl, just configured slightly differently."[88] Thus it is questionable whether zoning has made an appreciable difference in the way in which the suburbs were developed.

Zoning ordinances are ill-suited for land-use problems that are regional or even national in nature. Robert Nelson, a fellow at the Competitive Enterprise Institute, argued that locally based zoning was bound to fail:

> Although the planning and zoning theorists of the time considered that the metropolitan area or other large region was the appropriate jurisdiction for achieving coordinated land development, the tradition of local independence in land-use matters was too strong to overcome. Planning and zoning for the next forty years would be municipal. When planners pointed out that the actions of one municipality would often

FROM THE BENCH

"Zoning Out" the Mentally Retarded: *City of Cleburne, Texas v. Cleburne Living Center*

The owners of the Cleburne Living Center asked the city council of Cleburne, Texas, for permission to establish a group home for the mentally retarded. The proposed location was within Zone R-3, an "apartment house district," where permitted uses included apartments, fraternity and sorority houses, hospitals, and private clubs. The ordinance also required a special-use permit for "hospitals for the feeble-minded," a classification that included the living center.

Council members denied the living center a special-use permit, in part because neighbors disliked retarded individuals and were afraid of what would happen if a group home opened near them. The living center sued the city, arguing that the zoning ordinance discriminated against the retarded and therefore denied them equal protection of the law.

The case reached the United States Supreme Court, which, in *City of Cleburne, Texas v. Cleburne Living Center*, 473 U.S. 432 (1985), ruled unanimously that the city denied residents of the living center equal protection of the law. Although the justices disagreed on the level of scrutiny that should be given to the ordinance, they subjected it to a higher level of scrutiny than zoning ordinances in general.

Justice Byron White wrote the judgment of the Court, but his opinion commanded only four votes, one short of a majority. Justice White found that laws that treated the retarded differently were not as objectionable as laws that placed members of races or religions on a different legal footing. As a result, he concluded that the zoning ordinance should receive only minimal scrutiny from

be inconsistent with those of another, and that regional planning could never be truly effective as long as each locality acted independently of others, their arguments were to no avail.[89]

Zoning invites discrimination.

The American Planning Association defines "exclusionary zoning" as "zoning that has the effect of keeping out of a community racial minorities, poor people, or, in some cases, additional population of any kind."[90] Justice Morris Pashman, who wrote a concurring opinion in the *Mount Laurel* case, identified common

the Court. Applying that standard, he found that Cleburne's zoning ordinance was valid on its face.

Justice White concluded, however, that the ordinance was unconstitutional as applied to the living center because the city did not require a special-use permit for comparable living arrangements. He found that the city's decision to deny a permit was based on prejudice, not on the actual impact of a group home:

> [The city's] concerns obviously fail to explain why apartment houses, fraternity and sorority houses, hospitals and the like, may freely locate in the area without a permit. So, too, the expressed worry about fire hazards, the serenity of the neighborhood, and the avoidance of danger to other residents fail rationally to justify singling out a home such as [the Living Center] for the special use permit, yet imposing no such restrictions on the many other uses freely permitted in the neighborhood.

In his concurring opinion, Justice Thurgood Marshall contended that laws that treated the mentally retarded differently than other citizens deserved a higher level of scrutiny than economic regulations that favored one class of businesses over another. He pointed out that the interest in question in this case was a retarded person's right to establish a home, a right that the Court had long considered fundamental. Justice Marshall also argued that the retarded had been subject to a "lengthy and tragic history," which included a denial of rights similar to that suffered by African Americans. He observed that Cleburne's zoning ordinance, which used the obsolete term "feeble-minded," was the product of an era when society flagrantly discriminated against retarded citizens.

zoning policies that, in his view, were either "inherently exclusionary" or invited abuse: minimum house size requirements, minimum lot size and frontage requirements, single-family only housing, restrictions on the number of bedrooms, prohibition of mobile homes, and putting too much land in industrial or other nonresidential zoning districts.

Zoning creates both winners and losers. The losers tend to be the poor and members of minority groups. After the riots of the 1960s, commissions that studied them cited zoning restrictions as one cause of substandard living conditions in inner cities that contributed to the unrest. The winners tend to be existing—and well-off—residents, whose property becomes more valuable because the supply of developable land is limited.

Although zoning restrictions result in a better "quality of life" for those who already live in a community, they make it more difficult for newcomers to join them. Professor Bruegmann compared Houston to Portland, Oregon, which has strict land-use controls:

> A higher percentage of newcomers to Houston than to Portland have been poor and members of minority groups. The fact that Houston has somehow managed to accommodate all of these new citizens and provide for them a median family income only slightly below that of Portland is an extraordinary achievement. In part it has been able to do this because of a permissive attitude about growth and land use that has resulted in land and house prices in Houston below the American urban average. For many families, the economic and social mobility seen in Houston are more important than the benefits of smart growth, as seen in Portland.[91]

Summary

Zoning, which began as a means to curb "noxious" uses of land, is now used to achieve a variety of goals that have little to do with protecting public health and safety. In some communities, zoning ordinances have been inconsistently enforced and even misused to benefit powerful developers or to exclude people who are considered undesirable. Some critics argue that zoning laws provide the public with minimal benefits compared with voluntary restrictions, that they are based on the obsolete concept of "top-down" planning, and that they benefit existing residents at the expense of newcomers.

Zoning Promotes Better Communities

I n *Village of Euclid, Ohio v. Ambler Realty Company*, the Supreme Court held that local zoning ordinances did not deprive property owners of due process of law. Justice George Sutherland, who wrote the majority opinion, explained that society had evolved to the point that land-use planning was appropriate:

> Until recent years, urban life was comparatively simple; but, with the great increase and concentration of population, problems have developed, and constantly are developing, which require, and will continue to require, additional restrictions in respect of the use and occupation of private lands in urban communities. Regulations the wisdom, necessity and validity of which, as applied to existing conditions, are so apparent that they are now uniformly sustained, a century

ago, or even half a century ago, probably would have been rejected as arbitrary and oppressive.[92]

Zoning was developed to cope with new problems brought about by prosperity and urbanization. Eighty years later, continued growth has led to new problems, such as sprawl, that the *Euclid* Court could not have anticipated.

Zoning serves the public good.

Attractive, livable communities do not happen by themselves. Herbert Smith, an expert in the field, compared the planning process to putting together a jigsaw puzzle: "Separately, each piece has a unique shape. No piece will fit with another unless the maker of the puzzle has planned for it to do so, and, when all the parts are in the right place, you have an orderly, coordinated, attractive picture. So it is with land development."[93]

Experts have known about the benefits of zoning for decades. A planning guide published in 1928 by the U.S. Commerce Department explained some of them:

> Every growing town or city with an agricultural or undeveloped belt around it not only needs good highway connection with the country, for example, but desires to forestall the strangling effect of ill-planned or unplanned suburbs. To some suburbs and towns the maintenance of clear roadways and good transit facilities which pass through other jurisdictions is of most vital importance. Inadequate approaches to an important bridge in one municipality may become an intolerable burden to the citizens of others. Objectionable uses of land in one community may adversely affect another, as in the case of slaughter-houses with their offensive odors, or of factories set directly next to a city residence district.[94]

More recently, New York's highest court explained how zoning restrictions advanced the common good. It observed that "the restrictions may be designed to maintain the general character of the area, or to assure orderly development, objectives inuring to the benefit of all, which property owners acting individually would find difficult or impossible to achieve."[95]

Zoning Ruled Constitutional: *Village of Euclid, Ohio v. Ambler Realty Company*

During the 1920s, the U.S. Department of Commerce drew up a model zoning ordinance, which a number of communities adopted. It was not clear whether these ordinances would stand up to a constitutional challenge, however. The uncertainty ended when, in *Village of Euclid, Ohio v. Ambler Realty Company*, 272 U.S. 365 (1926), the U.S. Supreme Court upheld the constitutionality of zoning.

The case began when Euclid, a suburb of Cleveland, adopted a zoning plan that restricted the use of property in three ways: maximum intensity of use (industrial was the most intense, agricultural was the least), height of buildings, and minimum lot size. That approach, in which permissible uses are spelled out, is known as "Euclidian" or "as of right" zoning.

Euclid's ordinance was typical of those of other communities. Enforcement was carried out by the building inspector. A property owner who disagreed with the inspector's decision could appeal it to the Board of Zoning Appeals, which met in public and kept a record of its proceedings. If zoning restrictions would cause practical difficulty or unnecessary hardship to the owner, the board could "interpret the ordinance in harmony with its general purpose and intent, so that the public health, safety and general welfare may be secure, and substantial justice done."

The Ambler Realty Company owned 68 acres of land in Euclid that it wanted to develop for industrial use. After Euclid passed a zoning ordinance, Ambler filed suit to prevent village officials from enforcing it. The company argued that, because the ordinance reduced the value of its land by more than two-thirds, it had been deprived of property without due process of law. The lawsuit reached the Supreme Court which, by a 6 to 3 vote, ruled in favor of Euclid.

Justice George Sutherland wrote the majority opinion. He concluded that the "general scope and dominant features" of the ordinance were a valid exercise of the village's police power. He added that zoning was a response to changes in the way in which Americans lived and analogized zoning ordinances to traffic regula-

Zoning improves quality of life.

At issue in *Euclid* was whether zoning ordinances had a rational relationship to the public welfare. Justice Sutherland listed some of the ways in which zoning benefits the public:

tions that would have been considered arbitrary in the days before automobiles. He also analogized the zoning ordinance to nuisance law and to building codes, both of which were valid forms of police-power regulation.

Although zoning ordinances were broader than earlier laws that regulated land use, Justice Sutherland concluded that they were not overly broad. He wrote that "the inclusion of a reasonable margin, to insure effective enforcement, will not put upon a law, otherwise valid, the stamp of invalidity" and added that "we are not prepared to say in the end that the end in view was not sufficient to justify the general rule of the ordinance, although some industries of an innocent character might fall within the [prohibited] class." Finally, Justice Sutherland noted that most state courts had found zoning ordinances constitutional and that some courts that originally struck those ordinances down later reversed themselves.

Ambler's challenge was one on the face of the zoning ordinance. In other words, it contended that the ordinance's mere existence violated its constitutional rights. Justice Sutherland left open the possibility that Euclid's ordinance, or that of some other community, might be found "arbitrary and unreasonable." That issue had not arisen in this case, however, because Ambler had not yet attempted to develop the land in question. He observed that the Court preferred to move slowly in extending constitutional principles to specific cases, especially "questions arising under the due process clause of the Constitution as applied to the exercise of the flexible powers of police, with which we are here concerned."

Two years later, a challenge to a zoning ordinance *as applied* came before the Supreme Court. In that case, *Nectow v. City of Cambridge*, 277 U.S. 183 (1928), the justices ruled that city officials had acted arbitrarily when they placed a portion of the owner's land in a residential zone.

The [state court] decisions agree that the exclusion of buildings devoted to business, trade, etc., from residential districts bears a rational relation to the health and safety of the community. Some of the grounds for this conclusion are promotion of the health and security from injury of children and others by separating dwelling houses from territory devoted to trade and industry; suppression and prevention of disorder; facilitating the extinguishment of fires and the enforcement of street traffic regulations and other general welfare ordinances; aiding the health and safety of the community by excluding from residential areas the confusion and danger of fire, contagion and disorder which, in greater or less degree, attach to the location of stores, shops and factories. Another ground is that the construction and repair of streets may be rendered easier and less expensive by confining the greater part of the heavy traffic to the streets where business is carried on.[96]

Property-rights advocates focus on the burdens of land-use restrictions but downplay the fact that those restrictions confer benefits on landowners as well. Richard Epstein, a law professor at the University of Chicago, provided an example, an ordinance that regulates the size and appearance of signs that businesses display:

Without the regulation, each individual has the incentive to make his sign as conspicuous as possible, because he will internalize all the gains from its prominent place and bear only a fraction of the associated aesthetic costs. Unilateral efforts to limit sign size will be of little use, as some people will exploit the opportunities created by others' self-restraint. Multiparty contracts cannot be negotiated, given the usual transaction cost constraints. A comprehensive ordinance can control the abuse, while guaranteeing each person the visibility needed for effective use of the signs.[97]

Glossary of Zoning Terms

Zoning has its own "terms of art"—that is, words or phrases that have a specific legal meaning. Being familiar with these terms will help you better understand the actions of your community's planning and zoning authorities. Here are some of the most important terms.

capital improvements plan: A list of the physical public improvements, such as roads, streets, and sewers, that are planned to be constructed over a multiyear period. The plan includes where the improvements will be located, when they will be built, and how they will be financed.

comprehensive plan (also referred to as a master plan, basic plan, or future land use plan): The documents created by the planning or zoning commission to guide the future growth and development of the community. The comprehensive plan is used as the basis for zoning regulations and decisions, subdivision regulations, and capital improvements.

legislative functions: Those zoning functions that are exclusively in the domain of elected officials. They include adopting the original zoning ordinance and later amendments to the ordinance and the community's zoning map.

nonconforming use: A use of the land that was lawful before the zoning ordinance was adopted and is therefore permitted to continue in the future even though current zoning regulations that apply to that parcel would not permit it to be established now.

planned unit development (PUD): A zoning technique that gives a developer flexibility in how land is used instead of forcing the developer to conform to the letter of the zoning ordinance. PUDs, which usually involve a large number of parcels, were created so that approval power would rest with elected local officials rather than with the zoning board. When a PUD is approved, specific standards must be clearly identified and reasonable in nature. Examples of the flexibility allowed in a PUD include situating homes on smaller than normally required parcels of land and then creating an adjacent park area for residents to enjoy and allowing a mixed use of a building so that professional offices or light-traffic commercial space can be built on the ground floor of residential buildings.

(continues on next page)

(continues from previous page)

practical difficulty: A criterion that must be satisfied before a zoning board of appeals may grant a "dimensional," or nonuse, variance. The general standard is whether strict compliance with restrictions that govern area, setbacks, frontage, height, bulk, or density would either unreasonably prevent the owner from using the property for a permitted purpose or would make it unnecessarily burdensome for the owners to comply with them.

quasi-judicial functions: Decisions by a zoning board of appeals that are similar to those made by a court. They include granting variances, interpreting the zoning ordinance, and hearing appeals of administrative decisions.

rezoning: The process of changing a zoning district from one classification to another.

self-created: A zoning problem created by the actions of the person who is applying for a variance. A self-created problem is not a basis for a variance.

site plan review: The process of reviewing site plans—drawings that illustrate the layout of land and proposed structures—to determine whether they meet the requirements of the zoning ordinance.

subdivision regulations: Regulations related to how land is divided. Their purpose is to ensure consistency with the zoning ordinance and to

The benefits flowing from regulation are referred to as "average reciprocity of advantage." A familiar example of average reciprocity of advantage is a *sidewalk easement*, the legal obligation of every homeowner in a neighborhood to allow the local government to lay a sidewalk along a strip of his or her property and allow the public to use the sidewalk. Although the homeowner's use of property is restricted, he also benefits from that restriction because he can walk throughout his neighborhood.

address basic public-service concerns such as sidewalks and access to public utilities.

unnecessary hardship: A standard that an applicant must meet in order to gain approval for a use variance.

use variance: A variance that allows a use of land on a parcel that is otherwise not permitted by the zoning ordinance. A use variance is typically granted when an applicant proves that no reasonable use can be made of the property under its present zoning classification.

variance: A specific authorization by the board of appeals to allow an owner to use a parcel in manner that would otherwise violate the zoning ordinance. There are typically two types of variances, use and nonuse. Nonuse variances deal with dimensional requirements such as setback, height, or area requirements.

zoning enabling act: A state law that authorizes local units of government to adopt and administer zoning regulations. Without these laws, local governments would lack the authority to use zoning to regulate land use.

zoning ordinance: An ordinance that regulates land use, adopted by the community's elected officials on the recommendation of the planning or zoning commission.

Oregon provides an example of how statewide land-use restrictions benefited the public. A 1973 law required communities to draw "urban growth boundaries" and to restrict the development of land outside those boundaries. Writer Rebecca Clarren explained the effect of that law:

In Lebanon, just seven miles east of Corvallis, the state's tenth largest city and home of Oregon State University, there are

> no cookie-cutter subdivisions, no Wal-Marts or Blockbuster
> Video stores, no snarling traffic along this main road. The
> sprawl that has come to define the periphery of so many of
> the West's urban centers just isn't here.[98]

She added that the law has protected farm and forest land:

> Washington state paves over 40,000 acres of forestland every
> year, according to a recent report by the U.S. Department of
> Agriculture. Western Oregon, where most of the state's tim-
> berlands are, loses only 1,000 acres of forest each year to urban
> and transportation development. . . . Because most forestland
> is off-limits to development, it stays in production. . . .

Although twice as many people moved to Oregon as to Idaho in
the past decade, Idaho traded more of its farmland for homes.[99]

Zoning protects the rights of individuals.

The expression that "no man is an island" applies to the exercise
of property rights. As the American Law Institute explained,
"Practically all human activities, unless carried on in a wilderness,
interfere to some extent with others or involve some risk of interference."[100] Herbert Smith offered examples of such interference:

> A neighbor, following the philosophy of doing what you
> please with your land, could decide that it would be nice for
> extra income to dismantle and rebuild junk automobiles in
> the back yard. Someone else could decide to turn his or her
> first floor into a discotheque and apply for a liquor license.
> Farther away, the so-called business district has grown into a
> poorly arranged hodgepodge, with commercial and industrial
> uses allowed to string out in strip configuration along the
> main traffic arteries.[101]

Smith also wrote that "things can and do happen that will
change our dream into a nightmare if no adequate protection

is provided by the strength of collective community action expressed through the legal tool of zoning."[102]

Zoning also "levels the playing field" between average citizens and powerful developers. In his dissenting opinion in *Dolan v. City of Tigard*, Justice Stevens argued that land-use restrictions, at least when applied to commercial property, should be viewed as a form of business regulation:

> The subdivider is a manufacturer, processer, and marketer of a product; land is but one of his raw materials. In subdivision control disputes, the developer is not defending hearth and home against the king's intrusion, but simply attempting to maximize his profits from the sale of a finished product. As applied to him, subdivision control exactions are actually business regulations.[103]

Land developers are in the forefront of the property-rights movement. The regulatory-taking measures that they support have the potential to dismantle zoning ordinances, while they stand to earn huge profits should they gain an unrestricted right to put land to its highest and best use.

Zoning promotes the rule of law.

Supporters of zoning ordinances argue that they protect the average citizen. They set out clear standards that govern what can be built and where. Proposals to change a community's zoning ordinance, rezone parcels of land, or grant a variance take place at public hearings at which citizens have the opportunity to comment. Planning and zoning boards must keep a record of their deliberations and explain the reasons for their decisions, and their actions are reviewable by courts. Zoning requirements also serve as a consumer-protection measure. For example, they require developers to provide adequate infrastructure such as sewer lines and to build homes that meet minimum quality standards. In the long run, those restrictions save homeowners a considerable amount of money.

Zoning is also flexible. It allows local officials to address new problems and to promote a broad range of social goals. New York's historic-preservation ordinance, which the Supreme Court upheld in the *Penn Central* case, was enacted because of

When Should Zoning Variances Be Granted?

General Criteria for Granting a Variance

- Strict compliance with area, setbacks, frontage, height, bulk, density, or other dimensional requirements would create practical difficulties, unreasonably prevent the use of the property for a permitted purpose, or make it unnecessarily burdensome to comply with the restrictions. The showing of mere inconvenience is not enough to justify a variance.

- Granting the variance would do substantial justice to the applicant as well as to other property owners in the district. Alternatively, granting a lesser variance than requested would give substantial relief to the applicant and be more consistent with justice to other property owners.

- The requested variance can be granted in a fashion that would be consistent with the ordinance will be observed and promote public safety and welfare.

- Exceptional circumstances apply to the property involved, or to the intended use of the property, that do not apply generally to other properties or similar uses in the same zoning district. The conditions that result in a variance request cannot be self-created.

- A variance is necessary for the preservation and enjoyment of the property rights of other property owners in the same zoning district.

- Granting the variance will not do any of the following:

  o Be materially detrimental to the public welfare or materially injurious to other nearby properties;

  o Increase the risk of fire or flood or endanger public safety;

  o Unreasonably diminish or impair the value of surrounding properties;

city officials' concern that "the standing of [New York City] as a world-wide tourist center and world capital of business, culture and government would be threatened if legislation were not enacted to protect historic landmarks."[104] Zoning has also been

- º Impair public health, safety, comfort, morals, or welfare;

- º Alter the essential character of the neighborhood; or

- º Impair the adequate supply of light and air to adjacent property or increase congestion on public streets.

Specific Criteria to Be Considered

- The size, character, and location of a development permitted after granting of a variance must be in harmony with the surrounding land use and must promote orderly development in the zoning district in which it is located.

- A development permitted by a variance may not make vehicular and pedestrian traffic more hazardous than normal for the district in which it is located.

- A development permitted by a variance must be designed so as to eliminate any dust, noise, fumes, vibration, smoke, light, or other undesirable impacts on surrounding properties.

- The location, design, and height of buildings, structures, fences, or landscaping permitted by a variance may not interfere with or discourage the appropriate development, continued use, or value of adjacent land or buildings.

- The development permitted by a variance must relate harmoniously in a physical and economic sense with adjacent land uses. In evaluating this criterion, consideration must be given to prevailing shopping patterns, convenience of access for patrons, continuity of development, and the need for particular services and facilities in specific areas of the community.

used to combat pornography. In *Young v. American Mini Theaters, Inc.*, 1976, the Supreme Court upheld a Detroit ordinance aimed at preventing the concentration of adult-oriented businesses in neighborhoods. Supporters of the ordinance argued that "the location of several such businesses in the same neighborhood tends to attract an undesirable quantity and quality of transients, adversely affects property values, causes an increase in crime, especially prostitution, and encourages residents and businesses to move elsewhere."[105]

It can be argued that zoning restrictions are the type of regulation that actually makes people more free. In "The Tragedy of the Commons," Garrett Hardin argued that, after people agreed to pass a law against robbery, they were able to devote more time to activities other than defending themselves against robbers.

Zoning is more effective than previous forms of regulation.

Before zoning, land use in many communities was controlled by private agreement. "Restrictive covenants," deed restrictions that applied to anyone who owned the property, dictated how the property could be used. During the era of deed restrictions, people could leave crowded inner-city neighborhoods with incompatible land uses and move to suburban neighborhoods at the city's edge, where restrictions protected them against industrial pollution and noxious land uses. A person who wanted to stop a neighbor's illegal use of land, however, could not do so unless he or she was willing to invest the time and money on a lawsuit. Zoning ordinances, in contrast, do not depend on private enforcement. As Professor Robert Bruegmann observed, "What most zoning did was to take these private tools, make them public, rationalize them, and extend them across the entire city."[106] He added that "one of the chief functions of zoning was to give a much larger part of the population the same kinds of control over their environment that the wealthy had always enjoyed."[107]

The Zoning Appeal Process

The zoning board of appeals (sometimes referred to as the ZBA or called the Zoning Board of Adjustment) is responsible for hearing appeals of administrative decisions made by municipal staff, interpreting the zoning ordinance, and considering requests for variances.

When the Board of Appeals Acts

- When a citizen appeals a decision made by the zoning department or zoning administrator for which an appeal to the board is authorized by ordinance

- When a citizen or public official asks for an interpretation of the zoning ordinance or zoning map

- When a property owner makes a formal application for a variance from a specific ordinance requirement

- When the community's elected officials delegate other duties to the board of appeals, such as ruling on requests to expand nonconforming uses

Procedural Steps

- A person, or public official, starts the appeal by filing the necessary form and paying any required fees. The form includes the address of the property, the sections of the zoning ordinance being appealed, and a description or narrative and drawings or pictures describing the property and the circumstances that the applicant would like the board to consider about the property in determining whether a variance should be granted.

- The application is reviewed for completeness.

- A public hearing is scheduled to review the application. If required by local ordinance, notice of the appeal and the

(continues on next page)

(continues from previous page)

hearing is published in a local newspaper of record and a written notice is sent to adjacent property owners.

- The board reviews the application, reviews the ordinance, listens to testimony from a member of the municipal zoning or building department, and allows the property owner to speak. Adjacent property owners and other members of the public who express interest are also allowed to make a brief statement to the board.

- The board makes a decision that includes whether or not to grant the variance. The motion is accompanied by findings of fact to support the board's decision.

Further Appeals

- State laws normally allow one additional appeal. Appellate court reviews are limited to a *de novo* review of the record made before the zoning board of appeals. In other words, the applicant is not allowed to present new evidence or testimony to the court.

- The court reviews the record and opinion of the board to ensure that it:
  - Complies with the Constitution and state law;
  - Is based on proper procedure;
  - Is supported by competent, material, and substantial evidence on the record; and
  - Represents the reasonable exercise of discretion granted by law to the board of appeals.

- If the court finds that the record of the board of appeals is inadequate to make the review or that there is additional evidence that was not presented to the board of appeals, it can order the board of appeals to hold another hearing. The board of appeals may then change or stand by its original decision. The record and decision of the new hearing must be filed with the court.

- The appellate court may affirm, modify, or reverse a decision of the board of appeals.

Supporters of zoning maintain that enforcing deed restrictions and filing lawsuits to stop nuisances resulted in less consistent standards than ordinances provide. Robert Nelson of the Competitive Enterprise Institute explained:

> Instead of individual decisions by judges in response to the particulars of each case, zoning represented the establishment by the legislature of a set of permitting standards in advance of any particular application to build. Zoning advocates contended that this approach was superior to nuisance controls in that clear guidance was provided ahead of time to prospective developers. A common policy thus was substituted for the many decisions of individual judges. Case-by-case decision making, it was alleged, exhibited wide and unpredictably judicial variability in the determination of a nuisance.[108]

In addition, a zoning ordinance in place gives an owner more certainty as to whether a particular use of his land would lead to legal problems.

Summary

Zoning has produced well-planned and livable communities for more than 80 years. Courts have long accepted it as a means to promote the public welfare and have also recognized that even those who are burdened by land-use restrictions benefit from them as well. The legal framework of zoning rests on clearly spelled-out standards, openness, and uniformity. Zoning also provides homeowners with greater protection than deed restrictions did. It also provides better legal remedies against alleged nuisances because it was costly to file lawsuits against offending property owners and judges sometimes handed down inconsistent decisions.

The Future of Private Property Rights

I n his opinion in *Kelo*, Justice Stevens advised property-rights activists that the fight against broad eminent domain powers should be waged at the state level, not in the federal courts. Thus, the *Kelo* decision hardly settled the debate over eminent domain, let alone the larger controversies over property rights and regulation. If anything, it intensified the debate. Scott Bullock, the lawyer from the Institute for Justice who represented Susette Kelo, insisted that the *Kelo* decision will be overruled. He wrote:

> I am confident that one day, perhaps in the not-too-distant future, the Supreme Court will reconsider and overturn its disastrous *Kelo* ruling, consigning it to the same fate as other discredited decisions like *Plessy v. Ferguson* (which upheld "separate but equal" treatment of the races) and *Korematsu v. U.S.* (which upheld the internment of Japanese-Americans during World War II).[109]

Condemnation in the Post-*Kelo* Era

As Justice Stevens noted in *Kelo*, many states already had public-use standards that were stricter than the Supreme Court's standard. In the wake of that decision, lawmakers moved quickly to pass laws that restrict *Kelo*-type condemnations, and, in the 2006 election, voters in a number of states approved similar restrictions. By one estimate, about 40 states have enacted new

Oregon's Measure 37

In the 2004 election, Oregon voters approved Measure 37 by more than a 3 to 2 majority. Measure 37, which is the first broad regulatory-takings proposal to become law, has been codified as §197.352 of the Oregon Revised Statutes.

If the government enacts or enforces a land-use regulation that has the effect of reducing the fair market value of the owner's property or any interest in it, subsection (1) of the statute requires the government to pay the owner just compensation. Subsection (2) provides that "just compensation" is the reduction of the affected property's fair market value.

Subsection (11)(B) defines "land-use regulation." The definition includes acts of the Oregon legislature, rules of the Oregon Land Conservation and Development Commission, and communities' master plans, zoning ordinances, land division ordinances, and transportation ordinances.

Subsection (3) lists land-use regulations that are not considered takings. They include restrictions on public nuisances; health and safety measures such as fire and building codes, health and sanitation regulations, and pollution-control regulations; and laws against pornography and nude dancing.

Subsections (4) through (10) set out the procedure by which a property owner can enforce his or her rights. The owner has two years from when a new land-use regulation takes effect or from when he or she is denied permission to improve the property to make a written demand for just compensation. If the government continues to enforce the regulation in question for 180 days after the written demand has been made, the owner may go to court to obtain compensation plus costs and attorney's fees. As an alternative to paying compensation, the government may choose to "modify, remove, or not to apply" the regulation and allow the owner to put the property to a use that was permitted at the time it was acquired.

Citizens of Ohio rally outside the statehouse in January 2006, encouraging the Supreme Court to rule in favor of protecting private property rights. The state supreme court later unanimously ruled that the state constitution barred a city from condemning property to further an economic-development project.

restrictions on eminent domain. Even before *Kelo*, some state courts were placing stricter limits on condemnation. In 2004, the Supreme Court of Michigan concluded that economic-development takings violated the public-use requirement of the state constitution and expressly overruled the 1981 *Poletown* decision.

A year after *Kelo*, the Supreme Court of Ohio decided *City of Norwood v. Horney*, in which it ruled unanimously that the state constitution barred a city from condemning property to further an economic-development project. Even before the court ruled, state lawmakers voted unanimously to halt economic-development takings through the end of 2006 and to create a task force to study eminent domain. In a case that was heard before *Kelo* was decided, Oklahoma's highest court ruled in *Board of County Commissioners of Muskogee County v. Lowery*, 136 P.3d 639 (Okla. Sup. Ct. 2006), that economic-development takings were contrary to that state's constitution.

At the federal level, the United States House passed H.R. 4128, the Private Property Rights Protection Act, in 2005. The bill, which died in the Senate, was aimed primarily at *Kelo*-type condemnations. It would have barred the federal government from using eminent domain to acquire land for economic-development projects and would have denied federal economic development funds to a state or community that carried out a *Kelo*-type condemnation. H.R. 4128 also would have curbed condemnations of land that belonged to a church or some other nonprofit organization. In recent years, some communities have attempted to condemn church property in order to turn it over to private businesses that would bring in more tax revenue.

Will *Kelo* Survive?

Although *Kelo* was decided by only a 5 to 4 majority and proved unpopular with Americans, it is unusual for the Supreme Court to overrule a decision—especially soon after it has been handed down. By custom, the Court follows the principle of *stare decisis*—Latin for "let things decided stand"—in order to lend stability to the law. When a majority of justices disagrees with an earlier decision, they are more likely to narrow its effect, create exceptions to the rule the Court laid down, or refuse to take its reasoning to its logical conclusion. Two new justices have joined the Court since *Kelo* was decided, but both of them replaced justices who dissented in that case. Furthermore, no other justice signed on to Justice Clarence Thomas's dissenting opinion, in which he argued for a literal reading of the public-use requirement. It therefore appears that, at least for now, the

"Takings Impact": Executive Order 12630

In 1988, after the Supreme Court signaled its willingness to consider some regulations "takings," President Ronald Reagan issued an executive order that directed federal agencies to consider the takings implications of their actions. A number of states impose similar requirements on their agencies.

Section 2(a) of the order defines "policies that have takings implications" to include legislation, regulations, proposed legislation or regulations, and federal policy statements that, if carried out, could be considered takings. Examples include the requirement of a permit to make use of property, conditions placed on property use, and requirements that owners dedicate part of their property to public use. "Policies that have takings implications" do not include the following:

- Actions that abolish regulations or reduce their interference with property use,

- Actions that affect property held in trust by the United States in connection with treaty negotiations with foreign countries,

- The seizure of contraband or the holding of property as evidence for an upcoming criminal trial,

- Studies and planning activities,

- Communications between federal agencies and state or local land-use planning authorities regarding proposed state or local actions,

- The placement of military facilities or military activities that involve the use of federal property alone, and

- Military or foreign affairs functions, other than the U.S. Army Corps of Engineers civil works program.

Section 3 sets out general principles of takings law:

(a) The actions of federal agencies are subject to the Takings Clause.

(b) An action may be considered a taking even if there is no physical invasion of property, the action results in less than a complete deprivation of all use or value, or the deprivation is only temporary.

(c) Merely asserting that a regulation promotes public health and safety does not avoid regulatory takings claims. Government action must address a real and substantial threat, "advance significantly" the public health and safety, and go no farther than necessary to achieve its goal.

(d) Undue delay in decision making or processing an application, during which the use of property is interfered with, can be regarded as a taking.

(e) Government action can be regarded as a taking even if no taking was contemplated.

Section 4 imposes specific requirements on federal agencies:

(a) When an agency requires an owner to obtain a permit in order to make use of his or her land, any conditions imposed on granting that permit must serve the same purpose that would have been served by prohibiting the use outright. The conditions also must "substantially advance" that purpose.

(b) Regulations that restrict the use of property must be proportionate to the overall problem that the restriction is meant to address.

(c) The time required to process an application for a permit or authorize the use of land must be kept to a minimum.

(d) Before taking action that would restrict the use of property, an agency must clearly identify the public health or safety risk that the restriction addresses, and establish that the restriction addresses that risk and is proportionate to it. The agency must also estimate how much compensation the government would have to pay if a court later rules that the restriction was a taking.

Section 5 requires the head of each federal agency to do the following: designate an official responsible for complying with the executive order, identify the takings implications of proposed regulations, and compile a list of regulations that resulted in regulatory-taking lawsuits along with a list of compensation awards resulting from those lawsuits.

condemnation debate at the federal level centers on *Kelo*-type economic-development projects.

Some members of the legal community believe that recent decisions are the beginning of a significant trend in constitutional law. In his dissenting opinion in *Dolan v. City of Tigard*, Justice Stevens expressed concern that the Supreme Court had begun to resurrect the substantive due process era of the early twentieth century, when property rights were paramount and judges were quick to invalidate laws that they found contrary to their definition of "liberty." Stevens and other liberals contend that judges from that era misread the Constitution and substituted their views of sound policy for those of elected lawmakers. Conservatives disagree. They accuse modern-day judges of creating rights that appear nowhere in the text of the Constitution and twisting the language of phrases such as "public use." Whose view of the Constitution wins out depends in large part on which political party controls the White House. Judges appointed by Republicans are more likely than those appointed by Democrats to take an expansive view of property rights and to view regulations as "takings."

Regulatory-takings Measures and Their Future

In the long run, regulatory-takings measures could be a more significant legal development than restrictions on *Kelo*-type condemnations. Regulations that limit land use have been a concern for years. In 1988, President Reagan signed Executive Order 12630, which required federal agencies to assess the "takings impact" of new federal regulations. That order did not limit the federal government's power to regulate, however, nor did it provide any financial assistance to affected property owners. In 1994, the Republican Party proposed a federal legislative agenda called the "Contract with America." That agenda included a broad regulatory-taking proposal that would have entitled an owner of land to receive compensation if a federal regulation reduced the value of the land by 10 percent or more. That proposal never won congressional approval, in part because the 10-percent threshold was low. Nowadays, proposed regulatory-taking measures typically set the threshold at 50 percent, and some versions limit the compensation requirement to specific governmental actions, such as denial of a permit to fill wetlands.

Generally speaking, state lawmakers have considered two approaches to protecting property rights. The first is regulatory-taking legislation that would compensate the owner when regulation reduces the value of his or her land by more than a certain percentage. So far only two states, Oregon (in 2004) and Arizona (in 2006), have approved such laws. Another, less drastic approach is "look before you leap" legislation inspired by Executive Order 12630. Those proposals would require the government to study whether a proposed regulation would be ruled a "taking," whether there are alternatives to the regulation, and how much it would cost the government if a court forced it to compensate property owners. Supporters argue that a "look before you leap" law would have saved South Carolina the millions of dollars it spent fighting David Lucas in court.

Like other innovative laws, regulatory-takings measures are an experiment, and voters might become disillusioned with them. Writer Ray Ring noted that some Oregon residents who voted to limit regulatory takings had second thoughts after feeling the law's effects. He wrote:

> The most poignant stories come from people who voted for Measure 37, and now see negative impacts on their own neighborhoods and property values. "I voted for the measure because I believe in property rights," Rose Straher, who lives in tiny Brookings on the southern Oregon coast, told me. The owner of a nearby 10-acre lily farm filed a Measure 37 claim

to turn it into a 40-space mobile-home park, and got the Curry County government to waive its regulations.[110]

A Marketplace Solution to Land-use Questions?

Free-market advocates believe that top-down regulation, especially with respect to the environment, has been a failure. They contend that regulators respond too slowly to new information

---

Ohio Justices Reject *Kelo*: *City of Norwood v. Horney*

A little more than a year after *Kelo* was decided, the Supreme Court of Ohio was faced with the same issue: Could the government condemn property for an economic-development project? The case began when Norwood, Ohio, a suburb of Cincinnati that had lost much of its industrial base, approved the replacement of a residential and commercial neighborhood with a $125 million project that consisted of offices, shops, and restaurants.

The developer persuaded most residents of the neighborhood to sell, but two couples held out. The city responded by taking steps to condemn their homes. It acted under an ordinance that gave it the authority to condemn property that was in a "deteriorating area," an area that was in danger of becoming blighted. The two couples filed suit to block the condemnations. The lower state courts refused to second-guess the city's determination that their neighborhood was deteriorating. In *City of Norwood v. Horney*, Nos. C-040683 and C-040783 (Ohio Sup. Ct., July 26, 2006), however, the Supreme Court of Ohio unanimously reversed the lower courts' decision.

Justice Maureen O'Connor wrote the majority opinion. She conceded that the Ohio courts had, over the years, read the Public Use Clause broadly. Even when an "incidental benefit" flowed to a private actor, courts allowed condemnations to go forward if there was "a clear public benefit" in the taking. She added that the concept of "public benefit" was broad enough to justify the condemnation of slum properties as a public-health measure: "In past cases, we found that the removal of blight alone conferred a sufficient public benefit to warrant the taking because the discrete act of removing blight served to remove an extant health threat to the public."

and often make decisions that result in greater costs to property owners than benefits to the public. Supporters believe that Adam Smith's "invisible hand" would be both fairer and more efficient. Professors James Rinehart and Jeffrey Pompe explained:

> Evidence demonstrates that private ownership and control of property under of a rule of law coupled with competi-

Justice O'Connor refused to equate clearing slums with redeveloping an area that was found to be "deteriorating," however. Although the Ohio courts had taken economic concerns into account in slum-clearance cases, she wrote that "we have never found economic benefits alone to be a sufficient public use for a valid taking. We decline to do so now." She added that a "deteriorating neighborhood" was not the same as a slum: "To the contrary, the buildings in the neighborhood were generally in good condition and the owners were not delinquent in paying property taxes. There is no suggestion that the area was vermin-infested, subject to high crime rates or outbreaks of disease, or otherwise posed an impermissible risk to the larger community."

Turning to the definition of "deteriorating area," Justice O'Connor concluded that it was so vague that it deprived affected property owners of due process of law. She noted that the definition "describes almost any city" and could apply to some of the most exclusive neighborhoods in America. In addition, she found that the criteria used to define a "deteriorating area," which included incompatible land uses, obsolete land-use planning, and "diversity of ownership," were highly subjective: "[W]e hold that government does not have the authority to [condemn] private property based on mere belief, supposition or speculation that the property may pose such a threat in the future." Justice O'Connor also concluded that the lower courts should not have deferred to the city's conclusion as to whether the neighborhood in question was a deteriorating area. Under the Ohio Constitution, she pointed out, it was up to the courts to decide what a "public use" was.

Finally, Justice O'Connor concluded that a provision of Ohio's condemnation statute, which barred the courts from halting condemnations, was unconstitutional, because it interfered with the inherent power of courts to preserve the status quo while a legal dispute was underway.

tive markets lead to the highest and most efficient use of resources. Since users deriving the highest benefits from a particular piece of land can repeatedly outbid other potential users, the property in question automatically goes to its highest and best use.[111]

One market-based solution that has become popular is "tradable permits" that allow businesses to buy the right to exceed pollution standards from low-polluting businesses. Gus DiZerega, a doctor in political science, explained how a tradable-permit system would make it easier to enforce environmental standards:

> If emission permits are bought and sold, polluters will have a powerful economic incentive to minimize their pollution and expose those polluting in excess of their permits. If I have a permit and you are polluting without one, or in excess of what you are allowed, the economic value of *my* permit falls.[112]

Another proposal, offered by John Baden and Tim O'Brien of the Foundation for Research on Economics & the Environment, is the creation of a "National Biodiversity Trust Fund." The fund would be financed in part by charging loggers, miners, and other people who extract resources from government-owned lands. Money in the fund could be used in a variety of ways, such as paying a "bounty" to landowners who provide habitat for endangered species. Professor diZerega explained, "People would want species to be listed and would create conditions on their land encouraging them to settle there and to reproduce. Rather than simply preserving relic populations, at least in some cases species could be put well on the road to recovery."[113]

Advocates also believe that market forces are more effective than regulatory approaches such as planning and zoning. Steven

Greenhut cited the example of Anaheim, California, which loosened its zoning restrictions in order to create a new downtown. He wrote:

> Anaheim created a land-value premium by creating an overlay zone that allowed almost any imaginable use of property. Because current owners could now sell to a wider range of buyers, the Platinum Triangle is booming, with billions in private investment, millions of square feet of office, restaurant and retail space, and more than a dozen new high-rises in the works.[114]

Anaheim also rejected the *Mount Laurel* approach to housing. City officials believed that market forces would be more efficient than court orders and fair-housing laws in making affordable housing available.

Should We Return to Common-law Principles?

Although they endorsed a free-market solution to land use, Professors Reinhart and Pompe also noted that an owner whose use of land harmed a neighbor could be sued under the common law. Supporters of the common law maintain that it has adapted well to a changing world and that it is also superior to regulation as a means of accommodating conflicting interests. Lynn Scarlett of the Reason Foundation provided a simple illustration:

> Consider an apartment building with a noisy air-conditioning unit that disturbs a neighbor. Asked for injunctive relief [a court order directing the apartment owner to stop disturbing his or her neighbor], the court may emphasize the neighbor's rights, requiring the apartment owner to eliminate the air conditioner noise—unless the neighbor agrees to some other arrangement. Or it may assign the owner the rights, declaring that the neighbor must put up with the noise unless he can make a deal with the owner. In

actual conflicts, injunctive relief usually balances the two interests.[115]

Roger Meiners, a professor at the University of Texas at Arlington, explained how common-law principles could be used to stop property owners from polluting the environment:

Are Environmental Laws Too Broad?
Rapanos v. United States

A common criticism of environmental laws is that their language is so broad that owners are forced to guess as to which land uses are permitted. One example is the phrase "waters of the United States," which appears in the Clean Water Act. Critics have argued that it has been stretched far beyond its original meaning, bringing millions of acres of land under burdensome land-use restrictions. A dispute over the meaning of that phrase came before the Supreme Court in *Rapanos v. United States*, No. 04-1034 (U.S. Sup. Ct., June 19, 2006).

The Clean Water Act requires owners of property that contains federally protected wetlands to obtain a permit from the Army Corps of Engineers before filling them. John Rapanos defied the law. He argued that the wetlands on his property were not covered by the act. Rapanos's case reached the United States Supreme Court. The justices concluded that the Corps of Engineers' definition of "waters of the United States," and by extension its jurisdiction over wetlands, was too broad. They failed to agree, however, on what the proper definition should be.

Four justices, led by Antonin Scalia, took a "textualist" approach that relied on the definitions of disputed terms. Taking that approach, Justice Scalia concluded that "waters of the United States" meant "continuously present, fixed bodies of water, as opposed to ordinarily dry channels through which water occasionally or intermittently flows." He argued that a broad definition could turn the federal government into a zoning board with authority over vast amounts of land. With respect to wetlands, Justice Scalia further concluded that only wetlands with "a continuous surface connection" to "waters of the United States" were governed by the Clean Water Act.

Four justices, led by John Paul Stevens, maintained that the Corps of Engineers had given the phrase "waters of the United States" a proper interpretation.

People owning land along rivers had the right to beneficial use of the water that passed their property. If an upstream user discharged damaging waste into the stream, without first obtaining permission from the downstream owner, then the downstream party had a cause of action against the polluter based on the tort of nuisance. When convinced by scientific

They took a "purposive" approach that rested on the intent of the Clean Water Act. The four justices criticized Justice Scalia for having placed artificial limits on the Corps of Engineers' regulatory authority. They argued that intermittent streams were as capable as carrying pollutants as permanent ones and that wetlands physically separated from a body of water still had the potential to affect the quality of water downstream. Justice Stevens also argued that the Corps was better qualified than judges to determine which wetlands fell within the scope of the Clean Water Act.

The deciding vote in *Rapanos* belonged to Justice Anthony Kennedy, who proposed an alternative to the Corps of Engineers' approach. He contended that there had to be a "significant nexus" between the wetlands in question and "waters of the United States" in order for the Clean Water Act to apply. Like Justice Stevens, he rejected Justice Scalia's requirements that bodies of water be permanent and that there be a continuous surface connection between wetlands and waters of the United States. On the other hand, he rejected Justice Stevens's deferential approach, which "would permit federal regulation whenever wetlands lie alongside a ditch or drain, however remote and insubstantial, that eventually may flow into traditional navigable waters."

Michael Dorf, a law professor at Columbia University, argued that the members of the *Rapanos* Court were not as intellectually consistent as they claimed to be. He suggested that terms such as "textualism" and "purposivism" can hide the justices' political leanings, and he added that "[i]n *Rapanos*, despite the jurisprudential thrusts and parries, the Justices really were fighting about the proper scope of federal environmental regulation."[*]

[*]Michael C. Dorf, "In the Wetlands Case, the Supreme Court Divides Over the Clean Water Act—and Seemingly Over How to Read Statutes as Well." FindLaw.com, June 21, 2006. Available online at http://writ.lp.findlaw.com/dorf/20060621.html.

evidence that the polluter had damaged the party down-stream, the court moved against the polluter. The offending party was generally ordered to cease polluting and to pay damages.[116]

Meiners believes that thousands of cases, filed by private par-ties acting in their own self-interest, would have produced fairer and more sensible rules than those imposed by regulators who enforce laws such as the Endangered Species Act. Furthermore, had we relied on the common law instead of legislation, our air and water would be cleaner than it is now. He explained:

> Recent advances in pollution control technology, advances in understanding the consequences of pollution, and changes in society's attitude about the acceptability of pollution would have led to a rule of strict liability under the common law for polluters, as has occurred in product defect law. Even in its limited role, the common law often sets standards far tougher than those set by statutes.[117]

Some argue that environmental laws have done more harm than good in yet another way: They actually protect polluters by limiting their liability and affording them the defense that their actions had been approved by regulators. Critics also argue that environmental laws are so complex that they are a "barrier to entry." In other words, start-up companies cannot afford the lawyers and experts that are needed to comply with those laws.

Summary
The Supreme Court's decision in *Kelo* intensified the debate over condemnation in particular and land-use regulation in general. Backlash against that decision led to a range of state-

level restrictions on *Kelo*-type condemnations, as well as similar legislation in Congress. These actions are part of a broader effort to provide owners with relief when the value of their property is diminished by regulations. Some scholars have proposed alternatives to the current regulatory approach to land use. Those alternatives include relying on free-market principles and falling back on long-established common-law rules to set land-use standards.

Introduction: Is Your Home Really Your Castle?

1 U.S. Const. amend. V.

2 *Mugler v. Kansas,* 123 U.S. 623, 661 (1887).

3 *United States v. Carolene Products Company,* 304 U.S. 144, 152 (1938).

4 *Hawaii Housing Authority v. Midkiff,* 467 U.S. 229, 240 (1984).

5 *Kelo v. City of New London,* 545 U.S. 469, 503 (2005) (O'Connor, J., dissenting.

6 Magna Carta, §39.

7 American Law Institute, *Restatement (Second) of the Law of Torts.* St. Paul, Minn.: ALI Publishers, 1966, §821D.

8 Ibid., §821B(1).

Point: The Government Abuses Condemnation

9 Peter Charles Hoffer, *Law and People in Colonial America.* Baltimore, Md: Johns Hopkins Press, 1992, p. 123.

10 *Poletown Neighborhood Council v. City of Detroit,* 410 Mich. 616, 646, 304 N.W.2d 455, 465 (Mich. Sup. Ct. 1981) (Ryan, J., dissenting).

11 Declaration of Independence.

12 Jay M. Feinman, *Law 101: Everything You Need to Know About the American Legal System.* New York: Oxford University Press, 2000, p. 211.

13 *Dolan v. City of Tigard,* 512 U.S. 374, 392 (1994).

14 *Kelo v. City of New London,* 545 U.S. 469, 517-518 (2005) (Thomas, J., dissenting).

15 Ibid., p. 17.

16 Poletown *Neighborhood Council v. City of Detroit,* 410 Mich. 616, 674–75, 304 N.W.2d 455, 478 (Mich. Sup. Ct. 1981).

17 Scott Bullock, Op-Ed, "The Specter of Condemnation." *Wall Street Journal,* June 24, 2006.

18 Edward D. Herlihy, Op-Ed, "Eminent Domain Hits the Links." *Wall Street Journal,* March 28, 2006.

19 Nicholas Kristof, "Road to Politics Ran Through a Texas Ballpark." *New York Times,* September 24, 2000.

20 Emily Chamlee-Wright and Daniel Rothschild, Op-Ed, "Government Dines on Katrina Leftovers." *Wall Street Journal,* June 15, 2006.

21 *United States v. General Motors Corporation,* 323 U.S. 373, 379 (1945).

22 Steven Greenhut, *Abuse of Power: How the Government Misuses Eminent Domain.* Santa Ana, Calif.: Seven Locks Press, 2004, p. 2.

23 *City of Norwood v. Horney,* 110 Ohio St. 3d 353, 355, 853 N.E.2d 1115, 1122 (Ohio Sup. Ct. 2006).

24 Charlotte Allen, Op-Ed, "A Wreck of a Plan." *Washington Post,* July 17, 2005.

25 Greenhut, *Abuse of Power,* p. 239.

26 Ibid., p. 242.

27 *Kelo v. City of New London,* 545 U.S. 469, 522 (2005) (Thomas, J., dissenting).

Counterpoint: Condemnation Promotes the Public Welfare

28 *City of Norwood v. Horney,* 110 Ohio St. 353, 361, 853 N.E.2d 1115, 1127-28 (Ohio Sup. Ct. 2006).

29 *Hawaii Housing Authority v. Midkiff,* 467 U.S. 229, 245 (1984).

30 *City of Norwood v. Horney,* 110 Ohio St. 353, 367, 853 N.E.2d 1115, 1132-33 (Ohio Sup. Ct. 2006).

31 *Kelo v. City of New London,* 545 U.S. 469, 482-83 (2005) (O'Connor, J., dissenting).

32 American Planning Association, *Policy Guide on Public Redevelopment.* Chicago: American Planning Association, 2004. Available online at http://www.planning.org/policyguides/redevelopment.htm.

33 Ibid.

34 Ibid.

35 National League of Cities, *Eminent Domain Examples* (last revised October 5, 2005). Washington, DC: National League of Cities, 2005. Available online at http://nlc.org/issues/more_issues/6235.cfm.

36 Ibid.

37 Ibid.

38 Testimony of Eddie Perez, Mayor of Hartford, before the Senate Judiciary Committee, September 20, 2005.

39 American Planning Association, Amicus brief in *Kelo v. City of New London*, 2005, p. 27.

40 Ibid., pp. 16–17.

41 Anthony Williams, Op-Ed, "Cities Need the Authority to Promote Economic Development." *The Day* (New London, Conn.), February 20, 2005.

42 Testimony of Eddie Perez, Mayor of Hartford, before the Senate Judiciary Committee, September 20, 2005.

43 Testimony of Bart Peterson, Mayor of Indianapolis, Before the House Judiciary Subcommittee on the Constitution, September 22, 2005.

Point: Land-use Restrictions Are Unjust to Property Owners

44 *Penn Central Transportation Company v. New York City*, 438 U.S. 104, 152–53 (1978) (Rehnquist, J., dissenting).

45 Robert Bruegmann, *Sprawl: A Compact History*. Chicago: University of Chicago Press, 2005, p. 213.

46 Roger Pilon, "Property Rights, Takings, and a Free Society" HARV J LAW PUB POL'Y 6:165 (Summer 1983) 187.

47 Nancie G. Marzulla, "Property Rights Movement: How It Began and Where It Is Headed," in *A Wolf in the Garden: The Land Rights Movement and the New Environmental Debate*, ed. Philip D. Brick and R. McGreggor Cawley. Lanham, Md: Rowman & Littlefield Publishers, 1996, p. 54.

48 Ibid., pp. 55–56.

49 James R. Rinehart and Jeffrey J. Pompe, "The *Lucas* Case and the Conflict Over Property Rights," in *Land Rights: The 1990s' Property Rights Rebellion*, ed. Bruce Yandle. Lanham, Md: Rowman & Littlefield Publishers, 1996, p. 97.

50 Ibid., p. 82.

51 Karol J. Ceplo, "Land-Rights Conflicts in the Regulation of Wetlands," in *Land Rights: The 1990s' Property Rights Rebellion*, ed. Bruce Yandle. Lanham, Md: Rowman & Littlefield Publishers, 1995, p. 106.

52 *Armstrong v. United States*, 364 U.S. 40, 49 (1960).

53 *Rapanos v. United States*, No. 04-1034 (U.S. Sup. Ct., June 19, 2006), p. 3.

54 Lee Ann Welch, "Property Rights Conflicts Under the Endangered Species Act: Protection of the Red-Cockaded Woodpecker." In *Land Rights: The 1990s' Property Rights Rebellion*, ed. Bruce Yandle. Lanham, Md: Rowman & Littlefield Publishers, 1995, p. 179.

55 Jesse Walker, "Specious Reform: Republicans Are Reforming the Endangered Species Act—But for Whose Benefit?" *National Review*, May 18, 1998, p. 36.

Counterpoint: Land-use Restrictions Are in the Public Interest

56 *Mugler v. Kansas*, 123 U.S. 623, 660-61 (1887).

57 *Penn Central Transportation Company v. New York City*, 438 U.S. 104, 134, fn 30 (1978).

58 *Lucas v. South Carolina Coastal Council*, 505 U.S. 1003, 1034 (Kennedy, J., concurring).

59 *Coates v. City of New York*, 7 Cow. 585, 605 (N.Y. Ct. App. 1827).

60 Joseph Sax, "Takings, Private Property, and Public Rights." YALE L J 81(2):149, 152, quoted in *Nollan v. California Coastal Commission*, 483 U.S. 825, 863–64 (1987) (Brennan, J., dissenting).

61 *Mugler v. Kansas*, 123 U.S. 623, 665 (1887).

62 Garret Hardin, "The Tragedy of the Commons." *Science* 162 (1968): 1244.

63 Ibid., p. 1245.

64 WorldWatch Institute, Getting the Signals Right: Tax Reform to Protect the Environment and the Economy. WorldWatch Paper No. 134. Washington, D.C.: WorldWatch Institute, 1997.

65 Environmental Defense Fund, *The Endangered Species Act: Facts vs. Myths*. New York: Environmental Defense Fund, 1999. Available online at http://www.environmentaldefense.org/article.cfm?contentid=1158.

66 *Rapanos v. United States*, No. 04-1034 (U.S. Sup. Ct., June 19, 2006) (Stevens, J., dissenting, p. 13).

67 Ibid., p. 14.

68 Ray Ring, "Taking Liberties." HighCountryNews.org, July 24, 2006. Available online at http://www.hcn.org/servlets/hcn.Article?article_id=16409.

69 Glenn P. Sugameli, "Environmentalism: The Real Movement to Protect Property Rights." In *A Wolf in the Garden: The Land Rights Movement and the New Environmental Debate,* ed. Philip D. Brick and R. McGreggor Cawley. Lanham, Md.: Rowman & Littlefield Publishers, 1996, p. 61.

70 Christopher Cooper, "Court's Eminent-Domain Edict is a Flashpoint on State Ballots." *Wall Street Journal,* August 7, 2006.

71 *Pennsylvania Coal Co. v. Mahon,* 260 U.S. 393, 413 (1922).

72 Robert Dreyfuss, "Grover Norquist: 'Field Marshal' of the Bush Plan." *The Nation,* May 14, 2006.

73 Sugameli, "Environmentalism," p. 66.

74 Ibid.

Point: Zoning Harms Property Owners and Provides Few Benefits to Society

75 Marzulla, "Property Rights Movement," p. 45.

76 Erin O'Hara, "Property Rights and the Police Powers of the State: Regulatory Takings: An Oxymoron?" in *Land Rights: The 1990s' Property Rights Rebellion,* ed. Bruce Yandle. Lanham, Md: Rowman & Littlefield Publishers, 1995, p. 57.

77 Pilon, "Property Rights," Harv J Law Pub Pol'y 6:165 (Summer 1983) 188.

78 *Penn Central Transportation Company v. New York City,* 438 U.S. 104, 140 (1978) (Rehnquist, J., dissenting).

79 Herbert H Smith, *The Citizen's Guide to Zoning.* Chicago: American Planning Association, 1983, p. 114.

80 Ibid.

81 Ibid., p. 125.

82 Greenhut, *Abuse of Power,* p. 50.

83 Jane Jacobs, *The Death and Life of Great American Cities.* New York: Random House, 1961, p. 14.

84 Bruegmann, *Sprawl,* p. 111.

85 Ibid., pp. 12–13.

86 Ibid., p. 106.

87 Ibid., p. 107.

88 Ibid., p. 190.

89 Robert H. Nelson, "Federal Zoning: The New Era in Environmental Policy," in *Land Rights: The 1990s' Property Rights Rebellion,* ed. Bruce Yandle. Lanham, Md: Rowman & Littlefield Publishers, 1995, p. 304.

90 Smith, *Citizen's Guide,* p. 223.

91 Bruegmann, *Sprawl,* p. 218.

Counterpoint: Zoning Promotes Better Communities

92 *Village of Euclid, Ohio v. Ambler Realty Company,* 272 U.S. 365, 386–87 (1926).

93 Smith, *Citizen's Guide,* p. 4.

94 U.S. Department of Commerce, Advisory Committee on Zoning, *A City Planning Primer.* Washington, D.C.: U.S. Department of Commerce, 1928, p. 14.

95 *Penn Central Transportation Company v. New York City,* 42 N.Y.2d 324, 329–30, 366 N.E.2d 1271, 1274 (N.Y. Ct. App. 1977).

96 *Village of Euclid, Ohio v. Ambler Realty Company,* 272 U.S. 365, 391 (1926).

97 Richard A. Epstein, *Takings: Private Property and the Power of Eminent Domain.* Cambridge, Mass.: Harvard University Press, 1985, p. 266.

98 Rebecca Clarren, "Planning's Poster Child Grows Up," HighCountryNews.org, November 25, 2002. Available online at http://www.hcn.org/servlets/hcn.Article?article_id=13540.

99 Ibid.

100 American Law Institute, *Restatement,* §827, comment b.

101 Smith, *Citizen's Guide,* pp. 5–6.

102 Ibid., p. 5.

103 *Dolan v. City of Tigard,* 512 U.S. 374, 401–02 (1994) (Stevens, J., dissenting).

104 *Penn Central Transportation Company v. New York City,* 438 U.S. 104, 109 (1978).

105 *Young v. American Mini Theaters, Inc.,* 427 U.S. 50, 55 (1976).

106 Bruegmann, *Sprawl,* pp. 105–106.

NOTES

107 Ibid., p. 106.

108 Nelson, "Federal Zoning," p. 304.

Conclusion: The Future of Private Property Rights

109 Bullock, "The Specter of Condemnation," June 24, 2006.

110 Ray Ring, "Taking Liberties," HighCountryNews.org, July 24, 2006. Available online at http://www.hcn.org/servlets/hcn.Article?article_id=16409.

111 Rinehart and Pompe, "The *Lucas* Case," p. 72.

112 Gus diZerega, "Environmentalists in the New Political Climate: Strategies for the Future," in *A Wolf in the Garden: The Land Rights Movement and the New Environmental Debate*, ed. Philip D. Brick and R. McGreggor Cawley. Lanham, Md: Rowman & Littlefield Publishers, 1996, p. 110.

113 Ibid., p. 112.

114 Steven Greenhut, Op-Ed, "The Anti-*Kelo*," *Wall Street Journal*, April 6, 2006.

115 Lynn Scarlett, "Evolutionary Ecology: A New Environmental Vision," Reason Online, May 1996. Available online at www.reason.com/9605/Fe.LYNNenviro.shtml.

116 Roger E. Meiners, "Elements of Property Rights: The Common Law Alternative," in *Land Rights: The 1990s' Property Rights Rebellion*, ed. Bruce Yandle. Lanham, Md: Rowman & Littlefield Publishers, 1995, p. 273.

RESOURCES //////

Books and Articles

Brick, Philip D., and R. McGreggor Cawley, eds. *A Wolf in the Garden: The Land Rights Movement and the New Environmental Debate.* Lanham, Md.: Rowman & Littlefield Publishers, 1996.

Greenhut, Steven. *Abuse of Power: How the Government Misuses Eminent Domain.* Santa Ana, Calif.: Seven Locks Press, 2004.

Hardin, Garret. "The Tragedy of the Commons." *Science* 162 (December 13, 1968): 1243.

Smith, Herbert H. *The Citizen's Guide to Zoning.* Chicago: American Planning Association, 1983.

Yandle, Bruce, ed. *Land Rights: The 1990s' Property Rights Rebellion.* Lanham, Md.: Rowman & Littlefield Publishers, 1995.

Pro-property Rights Organizations

The Competitive Enterprise Institute
www.cei.org
A research and advocacy organization that opposes government intervention in the economy and promotes free-market alternatives to regulation.

Institute for Justice
www.ij.org
A libertarian public-interest law firm that defends property rights and free speech against government regulators. The Castle Coalition (www.castlecoalition.org), an offshoot of the institute, is a national anti–eminent domain project that helps homeowners and small business owners who face condemnation.

National Center for Policy Analysis
www.ncpa.org
A conservative research and communications organization that favors free-market solutions to environmental problems and reform of laws such as the Endangered Species Act.

Pro-planning and Pro-environmental Organizations

American Planning Association
www.planning.org
A public-interest and research organization that encourages the use of planning and zoning to serve the public interest. Many of its members work in local government.

National League of Cities
www.nlc.org
The oldest and largest organization that represents the nation's cities and towns. It favors redevelopment, including the use of eminent domain when necessary, to revitalize communities and curb sprawl.

122

National Audubon Society

www.audubon.org
Focuses on birds and supports measures aimed at protecting them.

Natural Resources Defense Council

www.nrdc.org
Supports strong enforcement of existing environmental laws and favors new measures to control sprawl, global warming, and other threats.

Sierra Club

www.sierraclub.org
Supports environmental regulation and opposes efforts to weaken laws such as the Endangered Species Act.

Federal Agencies

U.S. Army Corps of Engineers

www.usace.army.mil
Responsible for developing and protecting the waters of the United States. Its jurisdiction includes granting permits to develop federally protected wetlands.

U.S. Environmental Protection Agency

www.epa.gov
The federal agency that enforces a wide variety of environmental laws, including the Clean Air and Clean Water acts.

National Marine Fisheries Service

www.nmfs.noaa.gov
Part of the U.S. Department of Commerce, the NMFS enforces the Endangered Species Act in regard to marine species.

The Fish and Wildlife Service

www.fws.gov
Part of the U.S. Department of the Interior, the FWS enforces the Endangered Species Act in regard to birds, animals, and freshwater species.

Provisions of the Constitution

Fifth Amendment

The Takings Clause places two restrictions on condemnation: It must be for a public use and the owner of condemned property must be given just compensation.

Fourteenth Amendment

The Due Process Clause in §1 of the amendment forbids a state to deprive a person of life, liberty, or property without due process of law.

Some state constitutions have language that places additional restrictions on the use of condemnation. One example is Article 10, §2, of the Michigan Constitution.

Cases

Berman v. Parker, 348 U.S. 26 (1954).
Upheld the use of eminent domain to redevelop a neighborhood, including individual parcels that were not blighted, and announced that the Supreme Court would not second-guess the government's decision to condemn property.

Dolan v. City of Tigard, 512 U.S. 374 (1994).
Expanded on *Nollan* by imposing an added requirement of "rough proportionality" between the condition and the state interest.

Hawaii Housing Authority v. Midkiff, 467 U.S. 229 (1984).
Upheld Hawaii's use of eminent domain to break up that state's highly concentrated land ownership and also stated that the condemnation power was as broad as the police power.

Kelo v. City of New London, 545 U.S. 469 (2005).
Reaffirmed the Court's long-standing policy of deferring to state and local officials' determination of what was a "public use" in condemnation cases but invited states to enact greater restrictions on eminent domain if they wished to do so.

Lucas v. South Carolina Coastal Council, 505 U.S. 1003 (1992).
Held that land-development restrictions that prevented an owner from building on his land amounted to a taking for which he or she should be compensated.

Mugler v. Kansas, 123 U.S. 623 (1887).
Held that a law that outlawed a previously legal business and greatly reduced the value of that business owner's property was a valid exercise of the police power and therefore did not deprive him or her of due process.

Nollan v. California Coastal Commission, 483 U.S. 825 (1987).
Held that, in order for a condition placed on the granting of a building permit to be constitutional, there must be a "substantial nexus" between that condition and a legitimate state interest.

Penn Central Transportation Company v. New York City, 438 U.S. 104 (1978).
Upheld a zoning ordinance that restricted the use of certain land but also stated that a regulation could interfere with the use of property to the point that it becomes a taking.

Pennsylvania Coal Company v. Mahon, 260 U.S. 393 (1922).
Stated that some regulations can "go too far" in limiting contract and property rights and thus amount to a taking.

Poletown Neighborhood Council v. City of Detroit, 410 Mich. 616, 304 N.W.2d 455 (Mich. Sup. Ct. 1981).
Gave the phrase "public use" a very liberal interpretation and allowed the city to condemn an entire neighborhood so that an auto plant could be built there. In 2004, more conservative justices who sat on Michigan's highest court overruled *Poletown.*

Southern Burlington County N.A.A.C.P. v. Township of Mount Laurel, 67 N.J. 151, 336 A.2d 713 (N.J. Sup. Ct. 1975).
Held that a local zoning ordinance that excluded low- and middle-income individuals violated the due process and equal protection clauses of the state constitution.

Village of Euclid, Ohio v. Ambler Realty Company, 272 U.S. 365 (1926).
Ruled that a local zoning ordinance, standing alone, did not deprive property owners of due process of law. Two years later, in *Nectow v. City of Cambridge,* 277 U.S. 183 (1928), the Court found that a community's enforcement of an ordinance was arbitrary and therefore unconstitutional.

Other Legal Materials

Executive Order 12630 (Volume 53, Page 8859, Federal Register, March 15, 1988). Requires federal agencies to examine regulations and other agency actions and determine whether they could be ruled a "taking" by a court.

Oregon Revised Statutes §197.352. The nation's first regulatory-takings measure, passed by a vote of the people in 2004. The law entitles a landowner to receive compensation in some cases in which land-use regulations or the actions of state or local officials have diminished the value of his or her property.

Terms and Concepts

average reciprocity of advantage
blight
Clean Water Act
common law
condemnation
dedication
Due Process Clause
easement
economic development
eminent domain
Endangered Species Act
environmentalism
exaction
exclusionary zoning
investment-backed expectation
"invisible hand"
just compensation
Kelo
land-use regulation

nuisance
planning
police power
precedent
property-rights movement
public purpose
public use
real property
regulatory taking
rule of law
slum clearance
sprawl
substantive due process
Takings Clause
"tragedy of the commons"
urban renewal
variance
wetlands
zoning ordinance

Beginning Legal Research

The goal of POINT/COUNTERPOINT is not only to provide the reader with an introduction to a controversial issue affecting society, but also to encourage the reader to explore the issue more fully. This appendix, then, is meant to serve as a guide to the reader in researching the current state of the law as well as exploring some of the public-policy arguments as to why existing laws should be changed or new laws are needed.

Like many types of research, legal research has become much faster and more accessible with the invention of the Internet. This appendix discusses some of the best starting points, but of course "surfing the Net" will uncover endless additional sources of information—some more reliable than others. Some important sources of law are not yet available on the Internet, but these can generally be found at the larger public and university libraries. Librarians usually are happy to point patrons in the right direction.

The most important source of law in the United States is the Constitution. Originally enacted in 1787, the Constitution outlines the structure of our federal government and sets limits on the types of laws that the federal government and state governments can pass. Through the centuries, a number of amendments have been added to or changed in the Constitution, most notably the first ten amendments, known collectively as the Bill of Rights, which guarantee important civil liberties. Each state also has its own constitution, many of which are similar to the U.S. Constitution. It is important to be familiar with the U.S. Constitution because so many of our laws are affected by its requirements. State constitutions often provide protections of individual rights that are even stronger than those set forth in the U.S. Constitution.

Within the guidelines of the U.S. Constitution, Congress—both the House of Representatives and the Senate—passes bills that are either vetoed or signed into law by the President. After the passage of the law, it becomes part of the United States Code, which is the official compilation of federal laws. The state legislatures use a similar process, in which bills become law when signed by the state's governor. Each state has its own official set of laws, some of which are published by the state and some of which are published by commercial publishers. The U.S. Code and the state codes are an important source of legal research; generally, legislators make efforts to make the language of the law as clear as possible.

However, reading the text of a federal or state law generally provides only part of the picture. In the American system of government, after the legislature passes laws and the executive (U.S. President or state governor) signs them, it is up to the judicial branch of the government, the court system, to interpret the laws and decide whether they violate any provision of the Constitution. At the state level, each state's supreme court has the ultimate authority in determining what a law means and whether or not it violates the state constitution. However, the federal courts—headed by the U.S. Supreme Court—can review state laws and court decisions to determine whether they violate federal laws or the U.S. Constitution. For example, a state court may find that a particular criminal law is valid under the state's constitution, but a federal court may then review the state court's decision and determine that the law is invalid under the U.S. Constitution.

It is important, then, to read court decisions when doing legal research. The Constitution uses language that is intentionally very general—for example, prohibiting "unreasonable searches and seizures" by the police—and court cases often provide more guidance. For example, the U.S. Supreme Court's 2001 decision in *Kyllo* v. *United States* held that scanning the outside of a person's house using a heat sensor to determine whether the person is growing marijuana is unreasonable—*if* it is done without a search warrant secured from a judge. Supreme Court decisions provide the most definitive explanation of the law of the land, and it is therefore important to include these in research. Often, when the Supreme Court has not decided a case on a particular issue, a decision by a federal appeals court or a state supreme court can provide guidance; but just as laws and constitutions can vary from state to state, so can federal courts be split on a particular interpretation of federal law or the U.S. Constitution. For example, federal appeals courts in Louisiana and California may reach opposite conclusions in similar cases.

Lawyers and courts refer to statutes and court decisions through a formal system of citations. Use of these citations reveals which court made the decision (or which legislature passed the statute) and when and enables the reader to locate the statute or court case quickly in a law library. For example, the legendary Supreme Court case *Brown* v. *Board of Education* has the legal citation 347 U.S. 483 (1954). At a law library, this 1954 decision can be found on page 483 of volume 347 of the U.S. Reports, the official collection of the Supreme Court's decisions. Citations can also be helpful in locating court cases on the Internet.

Understanding the current state of the law leads only to a partial understanding of the issues covered by the POINT/COUNTERPOINT series. For a fuller understanding of the issues, it is necessary to look at public-policy arguments that the current state of the law is not adequately addressing the issue.

Many groups lobby for new legislation or changes to existing legislation; the National Rifle Association (NRA), for example, lobbies Congress and the state legislatures constantly to make existing gun control laws less restrictive and not to pass additional laws. The NRA and other groups dedicated to various causes might also intervene in pending court cases: a group such as Planned Parenthood might file a brief *amicus curiae* (as "a friend of the court")—called an "amicus brief"—in a lawsuit that could affect abortion rights. Interest groups also use the media to influence public opinion, issuing press releases and frequently appearing in interviews on news programs and talk shows. The books in POINT/COUNTERPOINT list some of the interest groups that are active in the issue at hand, but in each case there are countless other groups working at the local, state, and national levels. It is important to read everything with a critical eye, for sometimes interest groups present information in a way that can be read only to their advantage. The informed reader must always look for bias.

Finding sources of legal information on the Internet is relatively simple thanks to "portal" sites such as FindLaw (*www.findlaw.com*), which provides access to a variety of constitutions, statutes, court opinions, law review articles, news articles, and other resources—including all Supreme Court decisions issued since 1893. Other useful sources of information include the U.S. Government Printing Office (*www.gpo.gov*), which contains a complete copy of the U.S. Code, and the Library of Congress's THOMAS system (*thomas.loc.gov*), which offers access to bills pending before Congress as well as recently passed laws. Of course, the Internet changes every second of every day, so it is best to do some independent searching. Most cases, studies, and opinions that are cited or referred to in public debate can be found online—and *everything* can be found in one library or another.

The Internet can provide a basic understanding of most important legal issues, but not all sources can be found there. To find some documents it is necessary to visit the law library of a university or a public law library; some cities have public law libraries, and many library systems keep legal documents at the main branch. On the following page are some common citation forms.

COMMON CITATION FORMS

Source of Law	Sample Citation	Notes
U.S. Supreme Court	*Employment Division* v. *Smith*, 485 U.S. 660 (1988)	The U.S. Reports is the official record of Supreme Court decisions. There is also an unofficial Supreme Court ("S. Ct.") reporter.
U.S. Court of Appeals	*United States* v. *Lambert*, 695 F.2d 536 (11th Cir.1983)	Appellate cases appear in the Federal Reporter, designated by "F." The 11th Circuit has jurisdiction in Alabama, Florida, and Georgia.
U.S. District Court	*Carillon Importers, Ltd.* v. *Frank Pesce Group, Inc.*, 913 F.Supp. 1559 (S.D.Fla.1996)	Federal trial-level decisions are reported in the Federal Supplement ("F. Supp."). Some states have multiple federal districts; this case originated in the Southern District of Florida.
U.S. Code	Thomas Jefferson Commemoration Commission Act, 36 U.S.C., §149 (2002)	Sometimes the popular names of legislation—names with which the public may be familiar—are included with the U.S. Code citation.
State Supreme Court	*Sterling* v. *Cupp*, 290 Ore. 611, 614, 625 P.2d 123, 126 (1981)	The Oregon Supreme Court decision is reported in both the state's reporter and the Pacific regional reporter.
State Statute	Pennsylvania Abortion Control Act of 1982, 18 Pa. Cons. Stat. 3203-3220 (1990)	States use many different citation formats for their statutes.

abandonment, 42–43
abuse, 28–32, 47–48, 71
alternatives, lack of,
    42–43
Ambler Realty Com-
    pany, 19–20, 86–89
American Mini The-
    aters, Inc., 98
American Planning
    Association, 41–42,
    45–46
appeals process, 88,
    99–100
arbitrariness, 55–57, 69,
    75–76, 83–84, 89
Arizona, 22, 44, 109
Arkansas, 49–50

benefits, costs vs., 33–36,
    57–60, 81–83
Berman v. Parker, 14–17,
    21, 26, 33–34, 38
blight, 16, 34, 35, 46, 75
*Bradley, Fallbrook Irri-
    gation District v.*,
    38–39
Brandeis, Louis, 53
Brennan, William, 58,
    62–63, 68–69
Bruegmann, Robert, 50,
    80–81, 84, 98
building restrictions. *See*
    land use restrictions
Bullock, Scott, 28, 29,
    102
buyouts, forced, 32

California, 76
*California Coastal Com-
    mission, Nollan v.*,
    18–19, 58, 62–63
*Cambridge (City of),
    Nectow v.*, 89
capital improvements
    plans, 91
*City of Norwood v.
    Horney*, 104–105,
    110–111

civil forfeiture, 65
civil rights, property
    rights as, 25
Clean Water Act,
    114–115
*Cleburne Living Center,
    City of Cleburne,
    Texas v.*, 82–83
Coasian solution, 72
Colorado, 34
common law, 19,
    113–116
commons, tragedy of,
    66, 72, 98
compensation, 27, 32–
    33, 44–45, 50–51,
    67–70, 103, 109
comprehensive plans, 91
condemnation, 32–33,
    42–47
condemnation power,
    14
Connecticut, 39, 40
conservation, 22, 49–50,
    57–60, 66–67, 112
constitutionality, 88–89
consumer protection,
    95–96
costs, benefits vs., 33–36,
    57–60, 81–83
covenants, 98–99

decisions, governmental,
    51–56
Delaware, 34
Detroit, 15, 24, 28,
    30–31
discrimination, 35–36,
    77–79, 82–84
Dolan v. City of Tigard,
    18–19, 59, 95, 108
dominant individual-
    ism, 62
drugs, 19, 47–48, 65

easements, 92
economic development
    projects, 12–13,

15–17, 26, 39–43,
    110–111
eminent domain power,
    14
enclosure, 72
endangered species,
    22, 49–50, 57–60,
    66–67, 112
environment, 114–115.
    See also endangered
    species
*Euclid, Ohio (Village of) v.
    Ambler Realty Com-
    pany*, 19–20, 86–89
exactions, 58–59, 63
exaggeration, 47–48,
    66–67
exclusionary zoning,
    77–79, 84
Executive Order 12630,
    106–109

*Fallbrook Irrigation
    District v. Bradley*,
    38–39
feudalism, 20–21
Field, Stephen, 65
Florida, 34
forced buyouts, 32
forfeiture, 65

General Motors Corpo-
    ration, 30–31
Georgia, 42–43
government, 32–33, 51–
    56, 71–73, 75–76
Grand Central Terminal,
    68–69
Greenhut, Steven, 21,
    28–29, 33, 35, 76, 80,
    112–113
Griswold, Oliver, 71
group homes, 82–83

Hardin, Garret, 63–66,
    72, 98
Harlan, John, 61, 63,
    64–65

Hawaii Housing Authority v. Midkiff, 14, 15, 20–21, 26, 38
Holmes, Oliver Wendell, 52–53, 71
Horney, City of Norwood v., 104–105, 110–111

Idaho, 94
incentives, financial, 44–45
Indiana, 47–48
individual rights, zoning and, 94–95

Kansas, 61, 64–65
Kansas, Mugler v., 18, 61, 63, 64–65
Kelo v. City of New London, 10–16, 25–28, 38–39, 41, 105–108
Kennedy, Anthony, 13, 62, 115
Kentucky, 43

Land Reform Act, 20–21
land use restrictions
as abuse of power, 19–21
arbitrariness and, 56–57
constitutionality of, 88–89
costs outweigh benefits of, 57–60
dangers of measures for, 67–71
exaggeration of impacts of, 66–67
future of, 108–110
New York and, 68–69
public interest and, 61–62
as taking, 18, 19, 50–51, 54–55, 68
legal principles, 38–39, 43–47, 95–98

Lucas v. South Carolina Coastal Council, 19, 53–54, 62, 109

Madison, James, 18
Magna Carta, 17–18, 51
Mahon, Pennsylvania Coal Company v., 18, 52–53, 71
Maine, 34
market forces, 63–66, 110–113
Marshall, Thurgood, 83
Marzulla, Nancie, 51, 52, 74
Measure 37, 67–70, 103
mentally retarded, 82–83
Michigan, 30–31, 98
Midkiff, Hawaii Housing Authority v., 14, 15, 20–21, 26, 38
mining, 18, 22, 52–53, 71
minorities, 35–36, 77–79, 83–84
Morris, Max, 16
Mount Laurel (Township of), Southern Burlington County N.A.A.C.P v., 20–21, 77–79
Mugler v. Kansas, 18, 61, 63, 64–65

N.A.A.C.P., 20–21, 77–79
Nectow v. City of Cambridge, 89
Nelson, Robert, 81–83, 101
New Jersey, 77–79
New London (City of), Kelo v., 10–16, 25–28, 38–39, 41, 105–108

New York City, Penn Central Transportation Company v., 18, 50, 68–69, 75–76
Nollan v. California Coastal Commission, 18–19, 58, 62–63
nonconforming use, 91
North Carolina, 56–57
Norwood (City of) v. Horney, 104–105, 110–111
nuisance, 19, 47–48, 53, 64–65, 75

O'Connor, Maureen, 110–111
O'Connor, Sandra Day, 15, 21, 26–27, 38
Ohio, 37–39, 88–89, 104, 110–111
Oklahoma, 46, 105
oligopolies, 21, 26
Oregon, 22, 50, 67–70, 84, 93–94, 103, 109

Parker, Berman v., 14–17, 21, 26, 33–34, 38
Pashman, Morris, 78, 83–84
Penn Central Transportation Company v. New York City, 18, 50, 68–69, 75–76
Pennsylvania, 42
Pennsylvania Coal Company v. Mahon, 18, 52–53, 71
Perez, Eddie, 45, 47
permits, tradable, 112
Pfizer, Inc, 11, 13
Pilon, Roger, 50–51, 75
planned unit developments (PUDs), 91
planning, 19–21, 80–81, 87–88. *See also* zoning

Poletown Neighborhood Council v. City of Detroit, 15, 24, 28, 30–31
police power, 58, 61–62, 64–65, 68, 71
pollution, 22, 72, 112, 114–115
Pompe, Jeffrey, 53–54, 55–56, 111–112, 113
population growth, 72
preservation, historic, 68–69, 96–97
private nuisance, 19
Private Property Rights Protection Act, 105
Prohibition, 18, 64–65
property rights, 25, 62–66, 74–75, 90, 102–105
public good, 63–66, 87–88, 110
public nuisance, 19, 47–48, 53, 64–65
public purpose, 12, 24, 27, 30
public use requirement, 21, 26–28, 30, 38, 58
public welfare, 37–38, 39–42

quality of life, 89–94

Rapanos v. United States, 67, 114–115
rational basis, 53
Reagan, Ronald, 22, 106, 108
reciprocity of advantage, 75–76
redevelopment plans, 16–17, 26, 40, 43
regulations. *See* land use restrictions
regulatory takings. *See* land use restrictions

Rehnquist, William, 25, 50, 59, 69, 75–76
restrictive covenants, 98–99
Rinehart, James, 53–54, 55–56, 111–112, 113
Ring, Ray, 67–68, 109–110
Ryan, James, 24, 28, 30–31

Sagebrush Rebellion, 22
Scalia, Antonin, 53–54, 57, 58, 114
Scarlett, Lynn, 113–114
self-created, defined, 92
site plan reviews, 92
"smart growth", 41
Smith, Herbert, 76–80, 87, 94–95
South Carolina, 19, 53–54, 62, 109
South Dakota, 34
Southern Burlington County N.A.A.C.P. v. Township of Mount Laurel, 20–21, 77–79
special interests, 28–32, 71
states
   measures for regulatory takings and, 67–71, 103
   protection of individual rights by, 109
   response of to takings, 25, 34, 70, 103–105
   role of, 27, 30–31
Stevens, John Paul, 12–13, 39, 55, 59, 67, 95, 102, 108, 114–115
subsidence, 52
substantive due process decisions, 53, 108
Sugameli, Glenn, 71, 73
Sutherland, George, 86–87, 88–89

Takings Clause, 13, 18, 24, 106–109
tax revenue, 34
Texas, 31–32, 82–83
Thomas, Clarence, 15–16, 27, 28, 35–36, 105
Tigard (City of), Dolan v., 18–19, 59, 95, 108
tragedy of the commons, 66, 72, 98
trespass, defined, 19

Utah, 34

variances, 76–80, 92, 93, 96–97

Wayne (County of), Hathcock v., 31
Welch, Lee Ann, 56, 57
welfare, 37–38, 39–42
wetlands, 57, 67, 114–115

Young v. American Mini Theaters, Inc, 98

zoning
   as abuse of power, 19–21
   appeals process and, 88, 99–100
   discrimination and, 83–84
   effectiveness and, 98–101
   exclusionary, 77–79, 84
   governmental misuse of, 75–76
   as harming property ownership, 74–75
   inconsistency of enforcement of, 76–80

lack of benefits from,
81–83
obsolete notions of
planning as basis
for, 80–81
promotion of better
communities by,
86–87

promotion of rules of
law by, 95–98
protection of individ-
ual rights by, 94–95
public good and,
87–88
quality of life and,
89–94

reverse spot, 69
terms used in, 91–92
zoning enabling acts, 93
zoning ordinances, 93

CONTRIBUTORS ////////

PAUL RUSCHMANN, J.D., is a legal analyst and writer based in Canton, Michigan. He received his undergraduate degree from the University of Notre Dame and his law degree from the University of Michigan. He is a member of the State Bar of Michigan. His areas of specialization include legislation, public safety, traffic and transportation, and trade regulation. He is also the author of seven other titles in the POINT/COUNTERPOINT series: *Legalizing Marijuana, Mandatory Military Service, The War on Terror, The FCC and Regulating Indecency, Tort Reform, Media Bias,* and *Miranda Rights.* He can be found online at www.PaulRuschmann.com.

MARYANNE NASIATKA is a writer and researcher based in southeastern Michigan. She received an undergraduate degree from the University of Notre Dame. She was a member of the Zoning Board of Appeals in Canton, Michigan, the state's fastest-growing township, for many years and chaired the board for four years.

ALAN MARZILLI, M.A., J.D., lives in Washington, D.C., and is a program associate with Advocates for Human Potential, Inc., a research and consulting firm based in Sudbury, Mass., and Albany, N.Y. He primarily works on developing training and educational materials for agencies of the federal government on topics such as housing, mental health policy, employment, and transportation. He has spoken on mental health issues in 30 states, the District of Columbia, and Puerto Rico; his work has included training mental health administrators, nonprofit management and staff, and people with mental illnesses and their families on a wide variety of topics, including effective advocacy, community-based mental health services, and housing. He has written several handbooks and training curricula that are used nationally and as far away as the territory of Guam. He managed statewide and national mental health advocacy programs and worked for several public interest lobbying organizations while studying law at Georgetown University. He has written more than a dozen books, including numerous titles in the POINT/COUNTERPOINT series.

DATE DUE

JAN   '10